Down with Gloom!

or

How to Defeat Depression

Jane

every good wish

"Down with PND"

love . Brice

Toronto June 1994

By BRICE PITT
Drawings by MEL CALMAN

Down with Gloom!

or

How to Defeat Depression

GASKELL

First published 1994
Reprinted 1994

Gaskell is an imprint of the Royal College of Psychiatrists, 17 Belgrave Square, London SW1
Published for the *Defeat Depression Campaign*, organised by the Royal College of Psychiatrists
in association with the Royal College of General Practitioners.

British Library Cataloguing-in-Publication Data
A catalogue record for this book is available from the British Library.
ISBN 0-902241-64-8

Distributed in North America
by American Psychiatric Press, Inc.
ISBN 0-88048-627-9

Publication of this book was made possible by the kind support of Boots Pharmaceuticals

Printed in Great Britain by Henry Ling Ltd, The Dorset Press, Dorchester

Contents

Preface

Depression. Black dog. Melancholia.
The blue meanies. Gloom!

Whatever we call it, there are far too many people who suffer from depression. They suffer either because they have the illness or because they are close to someone who does. Depression blights life. It makes every decision fraught, every action an effort. Life itself becomes a burden, and there are impulses to suicide. It is hard to think of a worse affliction than severe depression – it is 'Hell on earth'. Cancer, stroke, heart and lung disease, multiple sclerosis, motor neurone disease, if uncomplicated by depression are all more bearable.

In one vital respect, however, depression need not be so bad after all: it is highly treatable. But the tragedy is that not many people know this, so they do not seek help. Many, indeed, do not know that they are depressed: they think either that they are physically ill or morally deficient. Alas, too often their doctors fail to make the diagnosis for them. So there is a great deal of unnecessary suffering.

1991 was the centenary of what became the Royal College of Psychiatrists. To mark the occasion the College joined forces with the Royal College of General Practitioners in a major public education campaign: 'Defeat Depression'.

Depression was chosen because it is the most common, overlooked and treatable mental illness. The first year was given to discussions between the doctors about how to recognise and treat depression. This resulted in advice which was sent by the Department of Health to every general practitioner in England and Wales in 1993.

The second year of the campaign was aimed at the general public, and hence this book. Brice Pitt, the

Public Education Director of the Royal College of Psychiatrists, agreed to write it and Mel Calman, who has illustrated the College's series of 'Help is at Hand' leaflets, to do the drawings. Both Brice and Mel know what it is like to suffer from depression.

So who is this book for? Not really for people who are professionally involved with depression — they will know everything that is in it and a lot more.

Is it for people who are actually suffering from depression? Well, we certainly hope that some of them will somehow find a copy to hand when they are feeling down. It is not easy to read, or do anything much when you are deeply depressed, but we think Mel's drawings might catch the eye, and then some of what is written might be helpful.

What about those who know someone who is suffering from depression? Yes, we would certainly like them to read this book. It will help them to understand the nature of the problem, to listen sympathetically to the sufferer, to give appropriate advice — and to understand their own feelings.

But mainly this book has been written for the general public, the person in the street, the masses (if we are lucky!). Why on earth should they — you! — want to know about such a dismal topic? Because it is very important, because it is very interesting, because anyone can get depressed, and forewarned is forearmed. Anyway, these days — rightly — people want to know about matters concerning health as never before. Depression is not only one of the biggest health issues of our time, but one of the most misunderstood: our aim is to put that right. Also, we do not believe that to be serious we have to be solemn.

We would like to thank, in particular, Professor Robin Priest, Chair of 'Defeat Depression', Vanessa Cameron, Secretary, Deborah Hart, Public Education Officer, Jill Phillipson, Public Relations Officer and Dave Jago, Publications Manager of the Royal College of Psychiatrists for their encouragement, and Virginia Ironside for a thorough and very helpful critique of the first draft. Also, of course, the many sufferers from depression whose vivid descriptions of their plight have increased our understanding.

> "May I say, a happy issue
> Out of all your afflictions? I hope so."
>
> *(The Chaplain, 'The Lady's Not for Burning':*
> *Christopher Fry)*
>
> BRICE PITT
> MEL CALMAN

Acknowledgements

The list on p.70 is adapted from Aaron Beck *et al*'s *Cognitive Therapy of Depression* (New York: Guilford Press).

The quote on pp.72—73 is from *Psychogeriatrics,* by Brice Pitt. Reproduced by permission of the publisher, Churchill Livingstone, London.

The extract from Dr Zigmond and Dr Snaith's Hospital Anxiety and Depression Scale in Appendix 1 is reproduced by permission of the publisher, NFER-NELSON Publishing Company Limited, Windsor.

1 Introduction

We all get depressed, don't we? It's a part of life – you lose someone, you're disappointed, you get the hump. You get over it – time's a great healer, we've all got to go some time, there are plenty more fish in the sea. If it drags on, well, you've got to buck up, pull your finger out, haven't you – snap out of it, pull yourself together. You don't want to be a wimp, do you?

I've given up hope. I was never any good, and now I've been found out. I'm ruined and disgraced, it's all my fault. Of course, I'll go to prison – and a good thing too! I expect I'll be tortured and executed. I don't deserve to live. The sooner the world is rid of me the better. I'm in Hell, and that's where I'm going.

Many of us will agree with the first paragraph, and find the second quite bizarre. Yet the word depression applies to both – the normal sadness in a life which is bound to have its ups and downs, and the dreadful anguish which, fortunately, most of us are spared. Not surprisingly, people whose only experience of depression is the normal kind have little notion of the depths of misery to which the same word can apply.

Depressive illness is the modern term for such severe depression, but a better word was the old-fashioned melancholia. This comes from the ancient Greek for 'black bile', a term introduced by Hippocrates who suggested that our temperaments were composed of diverse 'humours', centuries before the birth of Christ.

History and literature give us many famous melancholics. In the Old Testament, Job says:

"Wherefore is light given to him that is in misery, and life unto the bitter in soul; which long for death, but it cometh not; and dig for it more than for hid treasures?"

In Shakespeare's *Merchant of Venice,* Antonio starts the play saying:

"In sooth I know not why I am so sad. It wearies me; you say it wearies you; but how I caught it, found it or came by it, what stuff 'tis made of, whereof it is born, I am to learn; and such a want-wit sadness makes of me that I have much ado to know myself."

Hamlet, early in the play, remarks:

"Oh that this too solid flesh would melt, fall, and resolve itself into a dew, or that the Everlasting had not fix'd his canon 'gainst self-slaughter! O God! God! How weary, stale, flat and unprofitable seem to me all the uses of this world!"

Although his father had just died, his mother and his uncle (her new husband) are impatient with his grief. The mother rebukes him:

"Cast thy nighted colour off — do not for ever with thy veiled lids seek for thy noble father in the dust. Thou know'st 'tis common — all that lives must die, passing through nature to eternity."

Such an attitude to those who seem to be depressed for no, or for too little reason is all too common still.

In *The Pilgrim's Progress*, John Bunyan gives so many vivid descriptions of severe depression, that he must surely have been writing from his own experience. Early in his pilgrimage, Christian falls into the Slough of Despond, from which he is eventually rescued by a man called Hope. Later he is imprisoned in Doubting Castle by Giant Despair, who urges him to suicide.

It seems likely that among those men and (in particular) women who were tortured, hanged, drowned and burnt as witches were many who were mentally ill with severe depression, readily confessing still more crimes than those of which they were accused.

Coming to the present day, many people were first made aware of depression when Arthur, in the popular 'soap' 'EastEnders' was a victim. The programme showed very well how wretched and perplexing the condition can be, but also how successfully it can be treated.

Famous people who very probably suffered from bouts of depression include the poets William Cowper and Samuel Taylor Coleridge, the composer Robert Schumann, the painter van Gogh, the writer Edgar Allan Poe, President Abraham Lincoln and Queen Victoria, whose prolonged mourning after her consort Albert's death earnt her the title of the 'Widow of Westminster' and almost provoked a constitutional crisis. Twentieth-century figures include the novelists Virginia Woolf and Ernest Hemingway and the poet Sylvia Plath, all of whom unfortunately took their own lives, the pianist John Ogden, the comedian Spike Milligan (who has recently written about his ordeal), the authors Graham Greene (who played a deadly game of 'Russian roulette' when he was very young and feeling very low) and William Styron (who has written a very vivid account of his depression in '*Darkness Visible*') and, of course, Winston Churchill, who referred to his depression as 'black dog', and was incapacitated by it for one or two years in his early career.

Here are some descriptions of what it is like to be severely depressed, by ordinary people.

"I have been 'took bad' and have passed through three days which have been like Hell on earth. I called the doctor out when I reached the edge – despite bumper doses of valium my panic was out of control. My face is going quite rotten, like me. Gone is the hope of a normal life, along with lots of other hopes. I have cancelled friends coming, told lies to get out of meetings and have serious thoughts about giving up my job."

Married physiotherapist, aged 31

"I don't like myself any more. I feel I don't belong. I want to hide myself in a corner and be invisible. I have hateful thoughts, and I'm so irritable. I used to be a coper — I've had a lot to cope with — but now I feel strange and out of place. I'm wasting everyone's time."

Housewife, aged 46

"I'm low all the time, as if my head's splitting. I can't be bothered with anything — too much trouble. After I wake up all the worries come on me. They call me a 'workaholic', but I'm not working now, just sitting indoors watching television — just looking at it, not really there. All my luck's gone; everything I touch seems to go wrong."

Scrap metal merchant, aged 62

"I've lost all interest in life. I don't want to live any more. I feel it's my fault. I'm fighting against being well. I'm tensed up and sick of everything. I want to stay in bed. I don't do the housework — I don't want to do anything, can't be bothered: I feel I want to run away from the house — get away from all the things I'm not doing. My face is old and my hair's not the same."

Then, on recovery:

"I feel as if I've been reborn — through the dark tunnel into the sunlight. I appreciate every little thing."

Housewife, aged 62

"Since I learned that my friend has cancer I've been obsessed with the idea that I must die of cancer too. Why should I be spared? It fills me with horror. I sometimes wish that I had it, so that it could be over with. I took an overdose a month ago to get it over with, but I don't know if I wanted to live or die. I feel paralysed by panic. I can't eat and I've lost 9 pounds. I don't feel like sex any more. I feel so guilty that I havn't been a loving daughter to my mother, nor a good mother to my son."

Housewife, aged 30

"I feel I have lost my will-power and am completely incompetent. My grasp of financial and technical matters is wanting, and my attention-span limited. I have more and more evidence of a failing memory. The thought of having to speak for, say, half an hour to some 50 people in the whole office on 'office procedures' terrifies me. I am sleeping badly although I feel tired in the late evening; I can usually get to sleep with the aid of tablets, but wake very early and cannot get back to sleep, and at that time my thoughts are at their blackest."

Architect, aged 56

"I feel ghastly. I can't get going in the mornings, I can hardly be bothered to take the dog for a walk, I don't want to meet anyone or even answer the phone. I realise that I'm a shit, and always have been. I have to face the fact that I've got a yellow streak. During the war, when I was Commanding Officer, I only flew missions every 8 or 9 days: it should have been every other day."

Former RAF bomber pilot, aged 71

"I was so looking forward to the baby – it seemed like everything I'd always wanted. But now – deep down – I wish I could give him away. I'm so utterly bloody miserable, and I just can't cope. John tries to help, but he doesn't really know what's hit him. I feel so inadequate – and such an ungrateful bitch. They all tell me he's a lovely baby, and I can see it – but I can't feel it."

New mother, aged 23

"I've been making an incredible amount of money. I've got this flat in Wapping, and a Merc and this really super girl. But all of a sudden it doesn't mean anything. It's as if the sun had dropped out of the sky. For the past month all I've wanted is to be dead – but I haven't the guts to do anything about it."

Commodities broker, aged 21

Why on earth should people get into these morbid states of mind? How common is depression? What can be done about it?

The following chapters will give the answers to these questions.

Spelling out the symptoms of depression

D despondency
  diurnal variation (mood changing through the
    day)
  doubt
  disenchantment
  delusions

E exhaustion
  enthusiasm (lost)
  enjoyment (lost)

P panic
  phobias
  physical symptoms
  pessimism

R retardation (slowing down)
  regret
  registration (difficulty in taking things in)

E eating disturbance

S sleep disturbance

S suicidal tendencies
  shame
  sex (loss of desire)

I irritability
  indecision
  inattention

O obsessions

N numbness
  negative thinking

2 What is depression?

The letters which spell 'D E P R E S S I O N' stand for many of its symptoms.

D

Stands for dismal, despondent, dejected, 'down', despairing, even doomed and, of course, for depression itself.

The mood in depression is typically one of sustained gloom. The past looks black, the future blacker, and the present offers no joy or comfort. In the worst states of depression, this misery is very severe and quite unrelieved for days, weeks, months and occasionally years: small wonder, then, that suicide seems quite thinkable! Often, though, even bad depression is a little more bearable in the afternoons and evenings, whereas the mornings are particularly dreadful; this is called diurnal variation, simply meaning variation in the mood through the day.

In milder depression, evenings are often the worst times. Also there are 'good days', but they are outnumbered by the bad, which are especially disappointing when a

Ah—time for my DEPRESSION!

WHY?
Why did she say that I'm DEPRESSED?
Everyone knows that I'm very cheerful.. If I thought for a minute that I was depressed.. I'd be very depressed..
ZZZZ..

good previous day had made it look as if things were at last coming right.

In very mild depression (fortunately the commonest form) there is still the capacity to be 'taken out of oneself', cheered up and even made to laugh, but, without such stimulation, life seems sad, grey, dull and empty.

D also stands for doubt. Depressed people doubt their worth, so that past achievements are dismissed: former glories seem to have turned to 'dust and ashes'. They are also disenchanted. The line from the old hymn *Abide with me*: "Change and decay, in all around I see" expresses the feeling very well.

Delusions occur only in the most severe forms of depression. Most people who suffer from depression fear, at times, that they are going mad, but in fact this is exceptional. There may, however, be delusions of guilt – "I'm the most wicked person in the world, I've committed the unforgivable sin", which sometimes give rise to paranoid delusions – "people avoid me, they talk about me, they all know how wicked I am, the police are following me, they all want to get rid of me, and quite right too!" Delusions of poverty are among the most common – "I'm ruined, bankrupt, destitute, I'll soon be in a workhouse, or on the streets." Sometimes there are quite weird delusions about the body's functions – "I'm blocked up", "I stink of decay", or even "I'm dead!"

E

Stands for exhaustion. Many depressed people greatly lack energy. They feel weary, worn out, drained, lifeless and everything is too much effort – physical as well as mental. Sometimes they are so weak and debilitated that they are sure they must be physically ill – with acquired immune deficiency syndrome (AIDS), myalgic encephalomyelitis (ME), leukaemia, a virus, heart disease or some other dread disorder – and believe that they are depressed because they are ill, or not ill because they are depressed.

E also stands for enthusiasm and enjoyment, which are virtually abolished by depression. Even people who are unaware of being miserable when they are depressed find that their usual pleasures and pursuits no longer appeal – including sex (see below). The medical term for this is anhedonia – a Greek word meaning 'inability to enjoy oneself'. Anhedonia is probably the most common symptom of depression.

Now what's on the Worry Agenda today?

P

Stands for panic – the most extreme form of the anxiety which often accompanies depression. Anxiety and depression are not the same thing – one indicates fearing the worst, the other the feeling that it has happened — but they frequently go together. Depressed people may wake in a state of panic, as they face the ordeal of the day ahead. Panic may also arise from phobias which sometimes complicate depression, notably agoraphobia — the fear of going out and about and meeting people. Crowded supermarkets, where decisions have to be made about what to buy, and where there is a long wait at the checkout, are especially likely to cause panic. Panics usually last no more than a few minutes, but severe depression is made still more terrible by agitation, which is like sustained panic — the sufferer is in a state of restless anguish, unable to keep still and often begging for help and reassurance.

P also stands for pressure on the head, palpitations and various pains (in the head, face, neck, back, chest and abdomen in particular), which are among the common physical symptoms of depression. These are not only distressing in themselves, but worrying as possible signs of serious bodily disease. One advantage of consulting doctors is that they can usually tell whether such symptoms are part of depression or not.

P is also for pessimism. People who are depressed expect the worst, and may do little or nothing to avoid it. Cognitive therapy (see Chapter 10) tries to overcome this 'power of negative thinking'.

R

Is for retardation, a state of slowing-up of thoughts, words and actions which, at its worst, means that some very depressed people hardly move or speak at all. When it is less severe, retardation gives the feeling of living life with the brake on. Depression is sometimes blamed on overwork. More often, however, depression causes overwork — it takes so much longer to get things done.

R is also for regret. Edith Piaf declared: "Non! Rien de rien! Non! Je ne regrette rien!" ("No, nothing! No! I regret nothing!"). People who are depressed, on the other hand, tend to regret everything. They 'weigh themselves in the balance, and find themselves wanting'.

R also stands for registration, the ability to take notice of things and commit them to memory. Preoccupied with their malaise and gloomy thoughts, depressed people tend not to notice everything that is going on and then worry because they cannot recall it.

Retardation aggravates the memory problem, which is certainly real, but it goes away when the depression lifts. Thinking the worst when depressed, however, people tend to conclude that they are suffering from Alzheimer's disease or some other form of dementia.

E

This time 'E' stands for eating. People who are depressed tend to lose their appetite, eat far too little and lose weight – one or two stone (6–12 kg) in a matter of months, or sometimes weeks. In very severe depression, especially in older people, there may be a total refusal to eat – or drink – at all: this creates a crisis, with danger of death.

On the other hand, mildly depressed people sometimes overeat, to comfort themselves. But if they get fat they have further cause for unhappiness and self-reproach.

S

Stands for sleep, of which those who suffer from depression feel they have far too little. This may be true – many go to bed late and wake early, at some ungodly hour like 4.30 a.m., after a night of bad dreams. They then feel at their very lowest ebb, and either lie sweating with 'the horrors' or drag themselves up into some form of activity as a distraction from their awful thoughts. Others have great difficulty in falling asleep, however weary they are when they go to bed. Others still want to find oblivion and *escape* from the wretchedness of being awake, so can never get enough

If only my DOCTOR hadn't told me sleeplessness was a symptom of DEPRESSION – I'd never have known I had it

calman

sleep. They have great difficulty in getting up in the morning, and want to hide away from the world in bed.

It was found that one lady who complained of early waking actually went to bed at 7 p.m. and woke at 10 a.m. — far too soon for her!

S

Also 'S', alas, stands for suicide, the worst possible outcome of depression. Not all the 4000 suicides every year in England and Wales are due to depressive illness, but too many are; one in seven sufferers from severe depression will eventually die from suicide. In the Department of Health's paper, *The Health of the Nation* (published in 1992), the aim is to reduce the number of suicides by 15% by the beginning of the next century, which demands a very determined effort to find and treat depressive illness more effectively.

Those who do not succeed in killing themselves may well do themselves harm, most often by taking an overdose of drugs (either prescribed or bought over the counter, such as aspirin and paracetamol, both very dangerous in overdosage). Some are 'failed suicides', others 'cries for help' without serious suicidal intent, but all need to be taken seriously.

Men are more likely to commit suicide than women, who are more likely to harm themselves. On the whole older people are more liable to suicide than younger, but at present there is a worrying increase in young men who kill themselves.

Even if they do not attempt or commit suicide, most seriously depressed people think about it a lot. They do not need to be asked about it to have the idea 'put into their head' — it is there already. The thoughts range from a desire not to wake up in the morning, through wishing to be dead, and ideas that the world would be better off without them, to contemplating ways and means. Most conclude that it would be too drastic, too devastating to those left behind, or that they are cowards, but in some, of course, the thought is father to the deed. It is quite wrong, incidentally, to claim that those who talk of suicide will not do it: the opposite is true.

S also stands for shame. When depressed, people are full of guilt. They rake over their past for memories of minor misdeeds — things they have and have not done — and judge themselves very harshly. It is as if the conscience becomes hypersensitive, critical and punishing. Severe feelings of guilt certainly aggravate the tendency to suicide.

S also stands for sex, which becomes of very little interest to most people who are depressed. This source of consolation is therefore lost for the time being, and the partner may feel hurt and rejected. Loss of sexual desire (or libido) is quite a sensitive sign of depression, and its return is a good indication of recovery.

I

Is for irritability – an unpleasant accompaniment of less severe depression which makes the sufferer extra hard to live with. One woman said "It's like having pre-menstrual tension all the time." Quite placid people become intolerant and quarrelsome. Sensitivity to noise is a special kind of irritability.

'I' also stands for indecision, which is very typical of depression and a great impediment to everyday activity. It becomes difficult to decide whether and when to get up, to wash, what to wear, where to go and what to do: to have 'Cornflakes' or 'Rice Krispies' for breakfast; to go by this route or that; what to buy. Even answering the door or posting a letter can seem too much.

'I' also stands for inattention. Depressed people find it hard to concentrate and give proper attention to what is going on around them which, as has been mentioned already, contributes to their complaints of a bad memory.

I'm IRRITABLE because I'm DEPRESSED – which only makes me MORE IRRITABLE!!

calman

O

Is for — well, not many depressive symptoms begin with this letter. However, a morbid obsession with some disgusting or oppressive thought or image, involving excretion, depraved sex, decay and death, occasionally adds to the horror of depression. The sufferer does not indulge himself with these thoughts — they come into his mind unbidden (like the silly tune or advertising jingle we sometimes cannot get out of our minds), and add to the needless fears of insanity by which many depressed people are afflicted.

Obsessive—compulsive neurosis, in which there are often fears of contamination leading to endless handwashing, or inability to leave the home without an elaborate ritual of checks on locks, taps and switches, is not the same as depression, but is often complicated and worsened by it.

N

Is for emotional numbness: even the ability to feel loving towards one's nearest and dearest is sometimes frozen in depression. Attachment to friends and family may be weakened, and this may help to explain how some desperately depressed people, even though they normally feel well-loved and cherished, can bring themselves to commit suicide.

N is also for negative thinking, which has been mentioned above. Depressed people come to see themselves as jinxed, as 'Jonahs', bringing ill-luck on themselves and those around them.

> 'It's foggy, there's a traffic jam, the train has been cancelled, I've got the toothache, that's typical of what happens to me all the time.'

An important part of treatment is to challenge such negative thoughts.

Diagnosis of depression

It is possible to have a few of these symptoms without being ill with depression. The diagnosis of the syndrome — the typical collection of symptoms indicating that someone has a depressive illness — depends on which particular symptoms someone has, and for how long they have had them. An American 'bible', used also by many people outside the USA, requires that, for the diagnosis of depressive illness, there must be depression (i.e. extreme sadness, misery, dejection) or loss of enjoyment of life, and four other symptoms, and that these must have been present for at least two weeks (not all that long, really) and cannot be explained by a recent bereavement.

Not many diagnoses are made after so short a time. Generally the syndrome has been present for several weeks – or even months – by the time it comes to medical attention – if it ever does!

Professor David Goldberg and colleagues in Manchester have calculated that for 100 people with mental disorder attending the general practitioner's (GP's) surgery, only 44 will have the disorder recognised by the GP, nine will be treated by psychiatric services, and only one or two will be admitted to hospital for treatment.

3 How common is depression?

Unfortunately, depression is very common. Between a third and a half of us will have been afflicted by it at some time or other in the course of our lifetime. At any one time, one person in seven or eight is significantly depressed. By 'significantly' we mean that their lives are blighted by misery, bordering on despair, regret, anxiety, loss of confidence, pleasure, self-esteem and, indeed, the will to live. Although, as has been shown at the end of the last chapter, general practitioners (GPs) may miss rather more cases of depression than they diagnose, they still find more than two million new cases in the UK every year! Of the 4000 suicides recorded in the country every year, 70% (almost 3000) are the consequence of depression.

Depression is probably quite common in childhood, though then it takes the form of disturbed behaviour, such as surliness, tearfulness, sleeping poorly, withdrawal and avoidance of school, rather than open statements of feelings, like "I'm so unhappy".

I thought I was too young to have insomnia ...

Many women are afflicted by a tense, irritable form of depression before they have their periods: depression contributes to the well-known (and well-loathed!) pre-menstrual syndrome, or PMS. It only lasts for a few days, and usually goes away when the period starts, but those few days can be hell for the sufferer – and those who live with her! And it returns every month, or at any rate, most months. Among others, Professor Anthony Clare has shown that women who get depression at other times are especially liable to PMS.

Another risky time for women is when they have had a baby. If a child is unwanted, or if the delivery is very painful and drawn-out, or if the baby is abnormal or stillborn, depression is very understandable. But otherwise childbirth is rightly regarded as a 'happy event'. Yet even when the baby appears to be very welcome and the labour has gone well, one mother in ten gets post-natal depression (PND) and finds the early months of her new motherhood distressing rather than joyful. She is dreadfully tired, irritable, cannot get to sleep, loses appetite or eats too much ('comfort eating'), does not enjoy sex, and feels very inadequate because she cannot cope. She remembers posters showing blooming mothers with bonny babies in the ante-natal clinic, and feels ashamed that she is not like them. This sense of shame often stops her from seeking help. She is afraid of being considered a bad mother, and may even cover up her true feelings when the health visitor calls, in case the baby might be taken from her. So the known cases of PND are only the tip of the iceberg.

Women seem to be more at risk of depression than men for most of their lives, especially between the ages of 35 and 45. Around the age of 50, of course, comes the menopause or change of life, which, like PMS, may aggravate any tendency to get depressed or even bring on depressive symptoms for the first time.

Social class seems to be associated with depression: people in the highest and lowest classes are most liable. The highest include those in the professions, who are likely to be well off but carry considerable responsibility. The lowest (and lowest paid) are unskilled workers, many of whom these days, of course, are also unemployed.

There is a tendency for some people to get depressed at certain times of the year, such as the autumn (seasonal affective disorder, or SAD). It is unclear whether any particular countries, cultures or races have more or less depression. Some do not have a word for 'depression' in their language, but that does not mean that it does not occur, under another name.

It is also unclear whether people are more likely to get depressed in old age. Younger people often feel that their elders have plenty to be depressed about, but

I thought I wasn't OLD enough to be depressed..

calman

it may not seem that way to older people who have weathered their 'three score years and ten', are glad to have survived so long, and look forward to being around for a good few more years yet! That said, some of the worst forms of depression occur in old age; but whether that is due to their age, or afflictions which often go with age, like being widowed and physically ill, is not always easy to tell.

4 Are you depressed?

There are many questionnaires which can tell how likely it is that someone is suffering from depression. They are called screening tests, because they do not actually diagnose depression, but indicate that it may be present, alerting the health worker – doctor, nurse, psychologist – to pay particular attention to people who have high scores. They are sometimes used in research – to find out how many people from a particular population may be depressed – or for very practical purposes, for example to find out which mothers who have recently had a baby may have PND (post-natal depression) without having to interview them all at length.

Usually people fill in these questionnaires themselves, either answering 'yes' or 'no' to up to 30 questions, or else indicating that they have a particular symptom (like 'feeling as if slowed down') 'not at all', 'sometimes', 'very often' or 'nearly all the time'. The questionnaires have to have been tested to see that they measure what

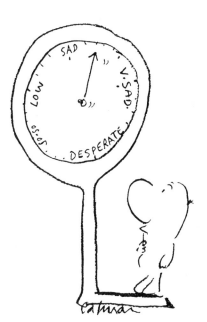

they are supposed to measure, that is the symptoms of depression (validity), and that when used by different testers, or at different times on the same people, they arrive at much the same score (reliability). So although most seem extremely simple, a lot of care has to go into their construction.

Some questionnaires are used for anyone who might be depressed. A good example is Dr Zigmond and Dr Snaith's Hospital Anxiety and Depression Scale (HAD) (see Appendix 1 for an extract from this scale).

As the name indicates, this scale measures anxiety as well as depression. Anxiety is not the same as depression (see Chapter 2 – What is depression) but the two often go together. All the even numbered questions (see Appendix 1) are about depression, and all the odd are about anxiety; the answers are scored by a qualified rater. Above a threshold score on either scale suggests that there may be depression or anxiety, needing further investigation with a view to treatment.

Some questionnaires are used for special purposes. The Edinburgh Post-natal Depression Scale (EPDS), developed by Professor John Cox, has ten questions about PND. It is given out to new (or once-again) mothers by health visitors and GPs, and has often helped to detect PND where otherwise it would have been missed.

Older people may have difficulty in reading the questions, and may also be hard of hearing. Reading the items to them aloud can strain the tester's voice and threaten the old person's privacy and dignity. So a special form of questionnaire (BASDEC – a funny name, which it would be boring to explain) has been produced, with statements about aspects of depression in large, bold print on a series of cards which the old person can sort into 'true' or 'false' piles quickly and easily. Seven or more cards in the 'true' pile suggest depression.

Questionnaires obviously have their limitations, but we have all got used to answering them for fun in magazines and newspapers, and it can be quite reassuring to a depressed person to see so much of what they feel down in black and white: at least they cannot be the only person in the world to feel that way.

5 Pictures of misery — the different kinds of depression

Over the years many people have tried to classify depression. Often they have divided it into two forms, but they have not always agreed on what those two forms should be. Here are some examples.

'Reactive' and 'endogenous'

'Reactive' means that the depression is a reaction to a very distressing event, while 'endogenous' means that it arises from within. The wife who takes an overdose after finding out that her husband plans to leave her for his secretary is 'reactively' depressed. The extrovert entertainer who becomes profoundly depressed for no obvious reason for two months every other year is 'endogenously' depressed.

The trouble with this division is that along with it goes the idea that reactive depression is wholly due to circumstances, and if those circumstances change for the better — if the unfaithful husband returns, loving and contrite — the depression goes. On the other hand, 'endogenous' depression is typical of severe depressive illness, with deep misery, worse at the beginning of the day, loss of appetite and weight, early waking and guilt, without the sufferer being able to say why they feel this way except to blame it on their inadequacy or sinfulness. Yet very often depression of this type is precipitated by an unhappy event, like bereavement, trouble at home or at work, or a physical illness.

'Reactive' depression is an extreme form of normal reaction, extreme either because the stress is overwhelming, for example when a man learns that his wife and children have been killed in a car crash, or because the distressed person has a low tolerance of stress and easily becomes overwrought. It comes on extremely quickly after the stressful happening, and lasts for as long as it takes the person to get over it – either because the stress has been relieved, or through eventually coming to terms with what has been lost. This is not a form of depression usually treated with drugs, except perhaps for brief sedation. Counselling, rallying family and friends and other practical supports are what is needed.

'Endogenous' depression is very likely to need a more 'medical' approach, as well as social and psychological approaches. But as, more often than not, it has been precipitated, if not adequately explained by, a 'life event' (usually, but not always, unpleasant – sometimes it can be brought on by winning the 'Pools'!), the term 'endogenous' is strictly incorrect. So you might have 'reactive' depression, 'reactive endogenous' depression, and purely 'endogenous' depression, which is more than a little confusing!

Further, only the depressed patient can know all the events which have brought about their depression, and they may not choose to disclose them. People do not necessarily tell their doctors everything. Imagine someone fearful of being found out after a secret act of adultery, incest, fraud or even murder! So 'endogenous' might not necessarily mean 'there's no obvious cause' but 'no obvious cause has been disclosed!'

'Neurotic' or 'psychotic'

This classification looks at depression in quite a different way. It tries to get away from the tricky question of what causes the depression, and looks at the clinical picture instead. It leaves out 'reactive' depression altogether, but retains the idea of 'endogenous' depression, now called 'psychotic', in contrast to another form called 'neurotic'. If we call someone neurotic we usually mean that they are 'nervy', worry unnecessarily, are full of fears and fancies and jump at their own shadow: it is not a very scientific term!

'Neurotic' depression, however, is not only milder than 'psychotic' but has a distinct, different pattern. It does not mean that the people who suffer from it are neurotic, though they may be. There are good days and bad, though more are bad.

The worst time of the day is towards evening. There may be overeating, for comfort, and weight gain. Sleep disturbance either takes the form of difficulty in getting to sleep or excessive sleeping. The depression is rarely of suicidal intensity, but is often associated with extreme irritability, mainly directed at the unlucky spouse or children. Such guilt as there is usually arises from this awful irritability.

'Psychotic' means that there is a serious derangement from reality, often involving hallucinations, such as hearing voices, and delusions, such as believing that everyone knows one's worst faults and is hostile in consequence. Very seriously depressed people show the kind of delusions of wickedness, poverty, decay and paranoia described in Chapter 2, and hallucinations which put those delusions into spoken words like: "We're going to put you in prison and throw away the key, you dirty slut!" Strictly, the term 'psychotic' should be reserved for people whose depression is so extreme that they are hallucinated or deluded.

The trouble with this classificationn is that while it looks fine on paper, people are not all that easily slotted into one category or the other. Some may show characteristics of both, at the same or different times. So many psychiatrists have given up this 'either/or' kind of classification and regard depression as a single illness which takes various forms.

'Bipolar and unipolar' (or 'manic—depressive or not')

Having said that, this is a division on which almost everyone can agree. To explain the terms, it is easiest to start with 'bipolar'.

The term 'poles apart' is helpful; the North pole is at the opposite side of the globe to the South, but they are both part of the same world. Depression is at one pole of what are called the 'affective disorders', or mood disturbances. The opposite pole is that of mania, in which there is a kind of wild jollity. Depressed people are 'low'; manic very 'high'. Depressed people are 'several degrees under'; manic 'way over the top'. Depressed people feel inadequate; manic are bounding with confidence, bursting with energy, and often feel inspired. They are forever on the go, talking 'nineteen to the dozen' about exciting new ideas and plans which they want to put into practice immediately. A normally shy, quiet young man admitted to hospital in a state of mania nipped out for the afternoon and returned having bought two expensive new cars and started a company!

The term 'pressure of talk' is used when manic people talk so fast, with so many topics crammed together, that they are almost incoherent. One thought may lead to another by a rhyme or pun:

> "I'm going for a walk, a talk, talk to me, why don't you, oh no, you're the shrink, but I'm shrink-proof, ha ha, the proof of the pudding is in the treating, 'ain't she sweet/ as she goes walking down the street - ay ay, a street walker, know what I mean, a bit of the other, eh?" and so, on and on.

If this is your MANIC phase — I dread your depressed one . . .

As the snatch of conversation shows, there may be bawdiness and undue sexiness, sometimes going on to thoughtless infidelity and promiscuity. Manic people spend money they have not got, and can ruin themselves or get charged with fraud, even though they had no intention to deceive. Although mainly cheerful and optimistic, they can be morose and irritable and even violent, especially when thwarted. They are deaf to reason, or would be if one could get a word in edgeways! They take no rest, eat too little, are impulsive and unpredictable, and altogether extremely hard to live with!

Mild mania, or hypomania, is a rather agreeable state in which some people can be more than usually creative and productive, genial, witty and entertaining, and very good company. Probably a number of comedians are at times hypomanic, like Spike Milligan who has recently written a book on *Depression and How to Survive It,* with Professor Anthony Clare (see Appendix 2). However, even hypomanic people may be at risk from their excessive optimism, which the harsh realities of life do not allow. Mr Micawber's expectation that 'something will turn up' served him well enough in *David Copperfield,* but is actually a disastrous philosophy for successful living.

The downside of hypomania, as of mania, is a tendency to get seriously depressed. Hence the other, more familiar term for 'bipolar affective disorder' – manic depression. Spike Milligan's book tells the story all too well. The depression in manic depression is just the same as the 'endogenous' depression already described. In manic depression, the mood disturbances occasionally occur at one and the same time ('mixed depression') but much more often in bouts lasting for weeks or months, with intervals of normality for a number of years, but an unfortunate tendency to recur. There may be several bouts of depression, then one of mania, or the other way about: the two poles of mood disorder do not necessarily alternate. Some very afflicted people are rarely normal, but either 'up' or 'down'.

Almost all sufferers from mania at some time or other suffer depression too, but most sufferers from depression will not experience mania. 'Bipolar' depression is less common than 'unipolar' (one-pole) depression, in which the person only ever suffers from depression. There is still a tendency for the depression to return after a while, and when it does it is just the same as the depression in 'bipolar' sufferers, but there is no tendency to mania.

'Agitated' and 'retarded'

These are two manifestations of severe depression. Retardation has already been discussed in Chapter 2. The sufferer is slowed in mind and body, takes a long time to answer any questions, uses few words and those few are uttered at length, with long intervals between them. There is no spontaneous talk, and in extreme cases there is no talk at all — the patient has become mute. Likewise, there is little or no spontaneous movement. The depressed person sits for ages in the same position, with a fixed expression of blank misery, and may barely be able to eat, drink or go to the lavatory. In extreme cases there is no movement — or speech — at all, no fluids or food are taken and life is seriously threatened.

Agitation is a state of appalling, restless anxiety with a craving for reassurance which cannot be accepted. Sufferers pace, wringing their hands, muttering, sighing, weeping and imploring, clutching at others for comfort and relief. "Help me, help me!" they beg: "I'm dying, I can't walk, I can't talk, oh please help me!" As they do not appear to be dying and can evidently walk and talk, they may get short shrift from insensitive attendants who brush them aside, step over their bodies when they collapse dramatically before them, and call them 'attention-seeking'; either they do not appreciate how desperate they feel, or they are embarrassed by not knowing what to do about it. Agitated depression must be the illness which brings people nearest to 'Hell on earth', and carries a considerable risk of suicide.

In milder depression retardation takes the form of inertia and lack of energy and motivation, and agitation is expressed as anxiety, unease and hypochondria, with excessive worrying about all sorts of physical symptoms and fears of heart disease and cancer.

'Masked' or 'smiling'

Sometimes people say "How can I be suffering from depression when I don't feel depressed?" This very reasonable question arises because it is possible to suffer from the syndrome of depressive illness without the symptom of depression (see Chapter 2). The depression may, in a sense, be masked by a physical symptom like pain in the face or neck. However, other symptoms like loss of enjoyment, interests, energy, appetite, weight and sleep enable the diagnosis to be made.

There are many physical signs of physical illness, like a rapid pulse, fever, swelling, a lump or a heart murmur. However, there are not many signs, as opposed to symptoms, of depression. One is loss of weight. Another is the facial expression, which often includes a straight mouth or one down-turned at the ends.

It is off-putting, then, when someone who is seen by a doctor for what seems like depression, smiles all the time. Perhaps they have that sort of face, or perhaps they have taken to heart that song 'Smile, though your heart is breaking'! (Although there may not be much gaiety in the eyes.) Anyway, a smile certainly does not rule out even quite severe depression. The traditional British 'stiff upper lip' or 'putting on a brave face' under duress can lead the unwary doctor to underestimate someone's suffering.

Sometimes a smile means:

"Things are all right now — at last I've decided what I must do — I'm going to take my life!"

'Dysthymic'

This American term is quite useful, because it describes a chronic, mild, grumbling kind of depression which most of us would recognise but for which we do not seem to have another word. It is defined as being depressed for most of the day, more days than not, for at least two years. The depression is accompanied by two of: poor appetite or overeating; under- or over-sleeping; fatigue; low self-esteem; poor concentration or difficulty in making decisions; and feelings of hopelessness. The depression would not have lifted for more than two months at a time over the two years. This might be regarded as 'chronic neurotic depression' (see above), but it is less likely to respond to drugs, and more due to personality and circumstances.

6 What causes depression?

We can divide this chapter into what predisposes to depression – what makes one person more likely to become depressed than another – and what precipitates depression – bringing it on in people who are, to a greater or lesser extent, predisposed.

Predisposing causes

Heredity

Does depression run in families? And if it does, is it in the genes which are passed on from one generation to another, or is it because of the way in which depressed parents bring up their children (that is, is it 'nature' or is it 'nurture'?).

The answer to this difficult question is usually provided by comparing the rates of illness in identical twins (who have, of course, identical heredity) with that in non-identical twins, who are no more alike than children of the same parents. Another method is to look at identical twins brought up by different parents, one or both being adopted (not a very common happening, as you can imagine). As identical twins have exactly the same heredity, it is not unreasonable to suppose that any differences they may develop under these circumstances are due to their upbringing. From studies of this type it looks as if:

(a) heredity is more important in bipolar (manic depression) then unipolar (no episodes of mania) depression
(b) it is more important in younger people than older.

So the younger the person, the more severe the depression and if there are episodes of mania, the more likely that heredity plays a part.

Personality

Some people are natural pessimists, very serious, not easily amused or 'taken out of themselves', and perhaps they are more liable to depressive illness than those who are more relaxed and have a sense of humour. Obsessional people who tend to be methodical, tidy, fixed in their views, creatures of habit and not good at adapting to changes in their circumstances seem also to be liable to depression — like the oak which breaks, rather than the reed which bends, before the wind. Obsessional people may be angry people who dare not show their anger, for fear that it would destroy others and themselves, so they keep it under tight control. One theory is that depression is 'anger turned inwards' (see p. 36).

A third kind of personality at risk of depression is cyclothymic — up and down, generally jolly, but with a tendency to gloomy spells — rather like manic—depression 'writ small'.

However, most people who get depressed are not too easily fitted into one of these three kinds of personality.

Losing one's mother in childhood

There is some evidence that people unfortunate enough to have lost their mother — through death, illness or her leaving home — when they are very young may be at extra risk of becoming depressed later in life. On the face of it, this makes sense. So devastating a loss might be seen as making the sufferer unable to bear much more later in life. On the other hand, coming to terms with so great a deprivation might have a 'toughening' effect, so that later losses were better tolerated — rather as a vaccination enables the immune system to withstand the ravages of smallpox.

Being a woman

Women are more likely than men to be diagnosed as depressed and admitted to hospital with depression. This may be because:

(a) they are readier than men to admit their feelings; men may feel that it is weak or 'wimpish' to do so
(b) male doctors, perceiving women as the 'weaker sex', might more readily diagnose them as depressed
(c) 'a woman's lot may not be a happy one'— a classic sociological study by Professor George Brown and colleagues in London showed that the people in the community most likely to be depressed were young mothers:

  (i) with three (or more) children under 10
  (ii) with an unsupportive partner
  (iii) with no one else in whom to confide

(iv) poorly housed

(v) having no employment outside the home.

Women are much more likely to get trapped in such a situation than men, although things are changing. There is some evidence that marriage is better for the mental health of husbands than of wives (and that when marriages breakdown the husbands suffer more than the wives).

(d) 'Vive la difference'! There are more fundamental differences between the sexes than that women have breasts, a vagina, womb and ovaries. Every cell of the body is different: men have an 'X' and a 'Y' chromosome, women two 'X's. Such differences affect the pattern of illnesses in the sexes. Of course men get cancer of the breast far less often than women, and women do not suffer any disorders of the prostate gland at all, but women are also at much less risk of heart disease until they reach middle age, and they outlive men by an average of five years: so much for the weaker sex!

The biological difference between the sexes most likely to contribute to depression is in the sex hormones, produced mainly by the ovaries in women from the time of puberty through menstruation and childbearing

until the menopause. The best known of these hormones are oestrogen and progesterone, and their levels vary a great deal – and have effects on the substances in the brain which may mediate depression (see monoamines, later in this chapter). Oestrogen is produced throughout the menstrual cycle, progesterone only during the ten days before a period, which may be relevant to premenstrual syndrome (PMS) and depression.

During pregnancy the levels of both hormones increase hugely, which may be why some women feel moody and dreamy when they are carrying. Then, once the baby is born, the levels drop very abruptly. One woman in two experiences a mild, brief mood disorder after giving birth – the 'blues' – while one in 500 suffers a very severe psychotic depression – which is more common than would be expected if childbearing had nothing to do with it: both these conditions typically begin on the third day after the birth, when the hormone drop might be expected to have its greatest effects.

The main hormone used for hormone replacement therapy (HRT) at and after the menopause is oestrogen, although some progesterone is given as well to prevent cancer of the womb. HRT is chiefly used to stop hot flushes and the thinning of bones (osteoporosis), but may also relieve some of the symptoms of depression which commonly develop at this time.

However, it is by no means proven that these hormone changes cause depression: the evidence is largely circumstantial. After all, all women experience them, but not all get depressed, and there is little to suggest that the changes are bigger in those who do: there have to be other reasons why some women might be more affected than others.

Further, there are social and psychological aspects to these times of hormone change. The woman who badly wants a baby, or who is very afraid of being pregnant might approach the time her period is due in tension and dread. The woman in two minds, at best, about whether she really wants a baby might be downcast when she actually has one. A baby is a heavy responsibility, very vulnerable and in need of feeding, changing, and a lot of attention and care. Some mothers do not at once take to their wrinkled, blotchy, scratchy, messy, demanding, crying and unresponsive infants, and feel burdened, bewildered and guilty that they are not more motherly.

The menopause is a milestone of ageing, a landmark signifying the end of reproductive life which some women regret. Their almost grown-up children may be untidy, erratic, surly, argumentative and a worry, or sometimes worse, leaving home while their parents are getting on and may be infirm and in need of care; even the husband may be abstracted and troubled, perhaps in the throes of a midlife crisis! One does not need to blame all these feelings on hormones, although they may well make a contribution. (See also below.)

Occupation

The main occupational risk of depression is unemployment. Suicide rates may be taken as a crude indicator of depression, and, in a time of recession, suicides among jobless younger men rise, until they overtake those of the notoriously suicidal old men. Boredom, lack of self-esteem and money worries are obviously depressing consequences of being out of work.

Again using suicide as a 'marker' for depression, the rates in doctors are well above the average: physician, heal thyself! Among doctors those most at risk are anaesthetists – who have ready access to a range of dangerous substances – and psychiatrists. Why? Perhaps it is partly because of isolation: in some ways it seems even more stigmatising to be a psychiatrist than to be mentally ill. Other doctors may be somewhat wary of them, and most psychiatrists dread being asked their occupation at a party because it either kills or distorts subsequent conversation. They are doomed to hear, for the nth time, all those killing psychiatrist jokes! They are often butts of the media, and, like social workers, 'damned if they do, and

damned if they don't' – they lock people up unnecessarily, and they release dangerous people too soon.

Possibly some psychiatrists, like other 'care givers', come into the profession seeking an answer to their own problems, but, to off-set that, many psychiatrists undergo psychotherapy in order to improve their self-knowledge and prevent any hang-ups from interfering with their understanding and treatment of their patients. Is it depressing to hear about other people's depression day in and day out? Not as a rule – psychiatrists are glad to have the opportunity to help – but on an off day it may get them down. Perhaps it is not very easy for one psychiatrist to turn to another and say "I feel terribly depressed" – but that is what is needed. Professor Kenneth Rawnsley, a former President of the Royal College of Psychiatrists, left a worthy legacy in the system he set up for sick doctors of all kinds to seek and get help.

'Learned helplessness'

If you find that whatever you do makes no difference to the unpleasant situation in which you find yourself, can that make you depressed? If telephoning and writing make no difference to the sequence of computerised letters you get from a council or a credit card company, asking for money that you have already paid, or persistently getting your circumstances and particulars wrong, you feel not only angry, but impotent, or helpless. Learning this, according to psychologist Dr Seligman, can indeed cause depression.

He started his studies on dogs, who learnt that whatever they did in an experiment they could not avoid a mild electric shock: they gave up, and eventually were so passive and demoralised that they were very slow to learn, if at all, a way of avoiding the shock when it was taught to them. Of course, dogs cannot say that they feel depressed, but can only act as if they might be. Seligman therefore extended the study to college students, who learnt, tediously and tiresomely, that whatever button they pressed they could not get a ****ing lift to stop for them when they wanted it! Consequently, they became mildly despondent. Seligman argues that when people are placed for a long time in a situation they can neither influence nor escape, like an old person being pushed from pillar to post in hospital or a refugee being passed from one camp or official to another, the chances of their becoming depressed are much increased.

Physical infirmity and illness

Physical infirmity, from conditions like arthritis, bronchitis, multiple sclerosis and Parkinson's disease, causes discomfort (pain and stiffness), disability (difficulty in walking), and consequently isolation (because of difficulty in getting about to meet people), dependency, insecurity (because it is always easier to rely on oneself than others, and the future is uncertain), and a greater or lesser degree of helplessness. It predisposes to depression, especially in old age.

'Anger turned inwards'

Babies can get furious, yelling their heads off and going scarlet in the face. Generally they are angry because they are hungry, uncomfortable and want a feed and a cuddle. Their anger can be quite alarming, even though they are so small. How much more terrifying may it be to them themselves! Babies are not sure about what comes from outside them or what from within them. Rage may feel like an overwhelming force, destroying everything.

According to one theory they realise, as they grow a little older, that the rage does come from inside them and is directed towards the person they need most, their mother. In a good, loving relationship the anger is softened and becomes manageable, but if things do not go so well the anger is turned inwards, for fear of its otherwise damaging the mother or provoking her into no less-damaging retaliation, say by withdrawing her love and care.

Sigmund Freud, who founded psychoanalysis, pointed out that the loathing which many seriously depressed people express towards themselves, makes more sense if it was originally directed, in childhood, at a loved person whose love was felt to have been lost: "hate knows no hate like love to hatred turned", as Alexander Pope put it. So there is a view that depression arises when this barely contained anger is aggravated by a further loss. This idea makes particular sense when one considers the phenomenon of suicide, which is a form of self-murder.

'The power of negative thinking'

Some people who do not think much of themselves expect little but still get downcast when events seem to prove them right! If bad things befall them they feel jinxed or accident-prone. If bad things happen to those around them they tend to take the blame, feeling like 'Jonah'. They were the children at school who would always blush when the head teacher asked assembly who was responsible for the graffiti in the girls' washroom, and would even submit to punishment rather than let the school be kept in, while the true culprit got away with it! If good things happen to them then it is a mistake — a fluke, they were not really entitled to such luck — and sooner, rather than later, they will have to pay for it! If they succeed they feel like imposters. If they fail, they feel it is only to be expected, but it gives

them no comfort. They agree with Groucho Marx, who said: "I wouldn't want to belong to any club which would have me as a member!"

Why should anyone be like this? Perhaps they were partly born that way, and partly made – by demanding, critical parents who take any successes for granted but are harsh on every form of failure. Under these circumstances there may well be 'anger turned inwards' and a considerable vulnerability to depression.

Brain and body chemistry

However psychologically minded we may be, we must accept that there can be no mind without a brain and a body, and that the functioning of that body is a matter of structure and biochemistry. It can be demonstrated with positron emission tomography (PET) that all our thoughts and feelings are accompanied by the use of oxygen and glucose in the brain. For a much longer period the electroencephalogram (EEG) has shown that the brain is electrically active. So let us look at some basic biochemistry and see what bearing it may have on depression.

Neurotransmitters

Nerve cells have a number of sticking-out processes – several short (dendrites) and one long (axon). These processes link up with the processes of other nerve cells, but there is a tiny gap between the end of one process and the beginning of another. This gap is called a synapse, and messages are passed from one nerve cell to another by chemicals, which are produced at the end of one cell's processes and stimulate receptors in the processes of the next. These chemicals are called, appropriately enough, neurotransmitters. They are fairly simple bits of proteins, known as monoamines.

There are a number of different neurotransmitters, including noradrenaline, serotonin and dopamine. People who are depressed seem to be distinctly short of these substances in their synapses, although whether they are always on the brink of being short, so anything that makes them still shorter readily makes them depressed, is uncertain. Antidepressants probably work by raising the level of monoamines in these synapses, by mechanisms explained in Chapter 11.

Hormones

The effects of sex hormones in women have already been discussed (see 'Being a woman' (d), p. 31), but there are other hormones produced by glands other than the ovaries of which too much or too little may cause depression.

Thyroxine is the hormone produced by the thyroid gland, and too little (the most extreme form of which is myxoedema) causes slowing of the body's processes which may be accompanied by psychiatric illness, often depression. Strangely, too much thyroxine (thyrotoxicosis) can cause depression, as well as anxiety.

The adrenal glands, perched on top of the kidneys, produce cortisone, but are under the control of the pituitary gland at the base of the brain. Too much cortisone (for example in Cushing's syndrome) can cause various psychiatric disorders, including depression.

Melatonin, produced by the pineal gland in the brain at night, may contribute to the depression of those who suffer from SAD (seasonal affective disorder; see Chapter 3).

The biological clock

Our bodies are adapted to the 24-hour day. Not only do we wake in the morning and go to bed at night, eat meals, and open our bowels at particular times, but the body chemistry varies throughout the day. In particular, levels of a hormone called cortisol, or hydrocortisone, produced by the adrenal glands under the influence of the pituitary gland in the brain are high in the mornings, and drop in the afternoon and evening; however, in depressed people they remain high all day. They even remain high in some depressed people despite attempts being made to suppress the activity of the pituitary with a synthetic hormone, dexamethasone. This led to a biochemical test for depressive illness, the Dexamethasone Suppression Test or DST. High cortisol levels go with stress as well as depression, so the stress of being depressed or the stress which causes the depression might both explain the high levels.

Some people tend to be 'larks' – at their best in the morning – others, 'owls', who come alive at night. 'Owlishness' in particular – not being at one's best first thing in the morning but improving as the day wears on – is like depression 'writ small' and might indicate a tendency to get depressed.

Drugs

It was the realisation that a drug for high blood pressure, reserpine, could cause severe depression which strengthened the 'monoamine' theory of depression, because it prevented the storage on the brain of three neurotransmitters: noradrenaline, serotonin and dopamine (see p. 38). Methyldopa, another drug for lowering blood pressure (although, like reserpine, not much used these days), can also be depressing. L-dopa, used in Parkinson's disease, may cause depression, even though it actually raises the level of the neurotransmitter dopamine. Steroid drugs, used for asthma, arthritis, arteritis and many other disorders, are like cortisone, and can cause depression. The contraceptive pill, which uses synthetic sex hormones, causes some women to become so depressed that they cannot take it any more. 'Beta-blockers', used to regulate the heart, lower blood pressure, and also to reduce physical symptoms of anxiety, may cause depression.

People who are dependent on alcohol (*Our Favourite Drug*, according to the Royal College of Psychiatrists) are at risk of depression – partly from the direct effects of alcohol on the brain and partly because of the difficulties in life which arise from the addiction, including unemployment, debt, loss of driving licence, sexual, marriage and health problems.

Precipitating causes

Loss

Losses of various kinds are far and away the most common causes of depression. The loss may be great or small, partly depending on how predisposed to depression the loser is.

Bereavement

It takes one to two years to get over the death of a loved person – in so far as one ever does – but during

I wish I could!

R.I.P.

that time the shock, disbelief, pain, resentment and preoccupation dwindle and there is a gradual detachment from the dead person and a return to the concerns of everyday life. This is what Freud called the work of mourning. Sometimes this work is not completed, and the bereft person is stuck at a stage when almost every waking thought is about the lost person who is felt still to be around and who is idealised:

> "He was such a wonderful man: no one could ask for
> a better husband. He was so kind and thoughtful.
> We never had a cross word."

Often such reminiscences are quite at odds with reality, which was that the couple led a cat-and-dog life. Out of such a denial of the truth of the relationship, or if the work of mourning gets stuck at a stage before the loss has been fully accepted, major depression may arise.

Actually old people seem to cope better with the loss of a spouse than younger people because the loss is expected – especially by women, who may be expected to outlive their husbands by five years if they are the same age, or longer if (as was the rule in earlier generations) they married an older man. If, however, the loss is of someone they had expected to outlive them, such as a child, their distress, as has been shown by Dr Klaus Bergmann, is much greater.

Bereavement does not only mean the loss of someone through death. Grief over lovers who have switched their affections elsewhere is made worse by anger, jealousy and hope: it is hard to complete the work of mourning for someone who is alive and just might come back. The loss of cherished hopes, such as for a scholarship or promotion, or of a job, especially in a recession when another will be hard to find, are also bereavements.

Acute physical illness

We know, of course, that we are mortal, but often act as if we expect to live for ever. This may be an advantage to us as a species – if we were acutely aware of our end at all times we might just give up! Such an awareness comes, however, if we have a brush with death, like a heart attack, or are suddenly disabled, for example by a stroke or an accident.

Depression is a major cause of disability after a heart attack, and can seriously delay recovery from illness. It can even cause death by removing the will to live – what old-time physicians called 'turning the face to the wall'. In old people physical illness is the most common 'trigger' for depression.

Viral infections

So often one hears the story that after, say, glandular fever, someone has been run down and demoralised for months. Influenza, from which nearly all of us must have suffered, leaves a feeling of weakness and debility for a week or two, and puts susceptible people at serious risk of getting depressed. Whenever there is a 'flu epidemic it is followed by a mini-epidemic of depression (as psychiatrists know all too well).

How does it happen? That is a good question, for which it is difficult to find a good answer. Viral infections challenge the immune system, which may be less effective in those who are liable to get depressed and still less so in those who are already depressed, so that depressed or potentially depressed people may be more likely to catch viral infections in the first place. This would explain a link between such infections and depression, but not why the depression more often follows than precedes the infection.

There was a view that infections could exhaust supplies of vitamin B_1 in the nervous system, so other treatments were often accompanied by vitamin supplements, but the value was never proven. Learning just how viruses make some people depressed could give a valuable clue to the biological (or physical) basis of depression.

7 What is the outlook?

The good news is that depression nearly always lifts, after weeks or months, even without any treatment.

It is always correct, as well as encouraging, to tell depressed people that their mood will not last forever, that they will get better, that time is on their side. Long before there were any specific treatments for depression it was recognised that people might suffer from melancholy moods ('the hump', for the more down-to-earth) which had to be endured but were phases which would pass.

The great German professor Emil Kraepelin observed in the last century that, in patients ill enough to be admitted to psychiatric wards, there was one illness which tended to be chronic and deteriorating – 'dementia praecox' (later called by the much more familiar name schizophrenia) – and another – manic depression – which proceeded in episodes, between which there was complete recovery. In such seriously ill patients, however, recovery could take a very long time. The distinguished Maudsley Hospital psychiatrist Dr Felix Post described how, in the days before electroconvulsive therapy (ECT), severe melancholic patients might have to be fed by a stomach-tube for years before at last the depression went away. Obviously tube-feeding could be dangerous as well as unpleasant: the food might go down the wrong way and cause choking.

The less good news is that depression has a tendency to come back. Recurrence is not inevitable – many people are only depressed once. But ever having been depressed is a 'risk factor' for being depressed again. How great this risk is varies a good deal. A very few people have recurrences so regularly that the timing of the next can be quite accurately predicted. As a rule these belong to the manic–depressive (or bipolar) variety of depression. Others may suffer, say, post-natal depression (PND) in their 30s, and then be all right for 40 years before becoming depressed again, perhaps after being widowed in their 70s.

A disorder recently identified by Professor Stuart Montgomery (of St Mary's Hospital, London) is recurrent brief depression: here the depression lasts only a matter of hours, or a day or two, but is extremely intense and returns several times in a year. It tends to happen in people with rather unstable personalities (always on a rather short fuse, and often getting into trouble because they act before they have thought things through) and unfortunately they are much at risk of impulsive suicide attempts.

Obviously it would be a very good thing to be able to stop depression from coming back. Some ways of trying to achieve this are discussed in Chapters 9 to 12.

Sometimes depression gets better, but not completely. Perhaps actual misery goes away, but the ability to enjoy life is reduced. There might be a tendency to bouts of mild depression, which was not there before. A spark is lacking, at home and at work. Sociability declines. Life seems to become more fraught, with fears of going out and about or concerning physical health, with many visits to the doctor. It used to be claimed that this sort of 'unresolved' outcome was more typical of depression developing in older people, but now there is evidence that it is quite common in younger people too. Another important task for treatment, then, is to try to ensure a more complete, as well as a more lasting, recovery.

Serious depression also reduces life expectancy. Study after study has shown that people with depression severe enough for psychiatric attention have a much higher mortality than those similar in every way except for being depressed. Why should this be? Suicide is an obvious answer, and depressed people are certainly at risk of suicide (see Chapter 2), but there are nowhere near enough suicides to account for all the premature deaths among depressed people.

A better explanation is that depressed people fail to take proper care of themselves. Depression leads to malnutrition, sometimes to alcohol abuse, failure to take medications needed for physical disorders (like high blood pressure, or heart disease) and loss of the will to live. In an important paper called *The Broken Heart,* Dr Colin Murray Parkes showed how people who had been widowed had a much increased chance of dying from heart disease during the year after their bereavement.

There is even the possibility that the immune reaction, which enables us to resist infections, is somehow diminished in depressed people (see 'viral infections', at the end of Chapter 6, p. 42). Those unfortunate melancholic people who were being tube-fed (see above) would have been at a great risk of dying from tuberculosis (which used to be rife in institutions, and unfortunately appears to be making a comeback), as well as of choking.

It is possible, too, that depression may affect the attitudes of doctors. In an enquiry into 'DNR', or 'do not resuscitate' orders in the case notes of older people admitted to the general wards of a London teaching hospital, it was found that the patients' mental state seemed to have more effect on the doctors' judgements than the severity of the physical illness. Dementia was especially likely to be associated with 'DNR', but so was depression.

Does good, effective treatment reduce the mortality from depression? For the particular episode, certainly; but for life expectancy afterwards? As yet we do not really know. It is an important area for research.

8   What is not depression?

Some conditions look like depression, but are not the same thing.

Depressive personalities

Older readers will remember the lugubrious charlady in the radio series 'ITMA' named Mona Lott whose catchphrase was "It's bein' so cheerful that keeps me going!" Mona was not suffering from clinical depression — she was one of Nature's miseries, and got a certain gloomy pleasure when her dismal predictions came true. Cassandra, the ancient Greek prophetess of doom (whom no one thanked for being right!) has had many natural successors. They include the cynics, the pessimists and the misanthropists, who usually find that their low expectations of mankind are fulfilled.

In Molière's play, *The Misanthrope,* the anti-hero Alceste is an angry, sardonic enemy to society's pretensions and hypocrisies, who takes pride in saying just what he thinks. By doing so, alas, he 'cuts off his nose to spite his face' and demolishes all hope of happiness with his lovely but flighty mistress Celimene. In *As You Like It,* Shakespeare created the most famous philosoper of melancholy of all, Jacques, who lives in the green wood with the banished Duke and his court and entertains them (and us) with his witty disenchantment, including the famous 'Seven Ages of Man'; he cannot share in the happy ending, but 'gets him to a monastery!'

Other mental disorders

Anxiety states

These are almost as common as depression. Anxiety often, but not always, goes with depression. Pure anxiety is a state of edgy apprehension, fearing the worst without always knowing what that worst will be.

Bodily effects of anxiety – palpitations, a dry mouth, overbreathing, dizziness, difficulty in getting off to sleep, a tight feeling in the pit of the stomach, frequent visits to the lavatory, muscular tension causing all sorts of aches and pains – naturally enough lead to fears of bodily disease. Sometimes these symptoms climax as panics. When these first happen the victim will often go to a casualty department, fearing a heart attack because of the sudden onset of palpitations, faintness and a tight feeling in the chest.

Anxiety states are often phobic – linked to special stressful situations like eating with other people or shopping in a supermarket. Whereas depressed people have lost the will to do these things, find the effort too much, and cannot see the point anyway, anxious people are held back by fear, which they would dearly like to overcome, if only they could.

Drugs have a much less important place in the treatment of anxiety than of depression. Psychological approaches work best.

Obsessions

These were described as occasional symptoms of depression in Chapter 3, but where they are very much to the fore they indicate an illness in its own right –

obsessive–compulsive neurosis. Examples of obsessions are the fear of having killed someone in the dark when driving a car. We can all understand that fear, but not how it could take over someone's life, especially when there is no evidence at all that any such thing has happened: the sufferer admits this, yet remains haunted by the mere possibility. Another obsessive fear might be of saying or doing somethimg quite outrageous in exalted company, like swearing in church, kissing the boss or doing a public striptease!

Fear of dirt and contamination leads to compulsive handwashing. It may be difficult to get out of the lavatory because of the notion of having touched a contaminated handle or surface after thorough washing. Checking is another crippling compulsion – did I turn the lights/gas/taps off? Did I lock the front door? This can delay a sufferer's leaving the house for two hours or more!

Obsessive–compulsive neurosis is often accompanied by depression, and while behavioural methods of treatment probably work best (in an essentially hard-to-treat disorder), antidepressants, notably those which increase the amount of serotonin available in the nerve-cell synapses of the brain, are also useful (see Chapter 10).

Eating disorders

Anorexia and bulimia – in which people (usually women) respectively starve and stuff themselves (or both!) are related to the idea of being the right shape and weight and not to being depressed. The weight loss in anorexia might suggest possible depression, but anorectics are not, as a rule, unhappy, although their families may well be. The anorectic is, indeed, achieving her aim of being ultra-slim, and all that concerns her is to get and stay that way. Antidepressant drugs do not help.

Bulimia takes the form of bingeing, followed by vomiting, using laxatives and attempts at starvation – although bulimic patients are much more likely to be of normal weight than anorectics. A number of bulimia sufferers also suffer from depression, and they may well be helped by treatment for depression as well as for the eating disorder.

Schizophrenia

Schizophrenia, one of the most devastating and most thoroughly misunderstood mental disorder, resembles depression to the extent that there is a change from the previous personality to becoming more stay-at-home, withdrawn and silent. However, people suffering from acute schizophrenia usually hear voices, talking to and about them, and often feel that they are under the influence of others who put alien thoughts into their minds. They are commonly deluded, feeling persecuted by the police, Masons, Jews, Irish Republican Army, or extraterrestrials, that they are undergoing a change of sex, or suddenly discovering that they have to save the world, like a new Messiah.

Sometimes seriously depressed people also hear voices and hold delusions, generally of being wicked, contaminated and about to undergo cruel punishment, but these are consistent with their deeply depressed mood and thus understandable. In schizophrenia, however, conversation is often very hard to follow, because one idea does not follow logically on from the last. As a rule, people who suffer from schizophrenia are much more odd than those who have depression. Their illness is also much more drawn out: some recover completely quite soon, but many others are never quite the same once they have been ill with schizophrenia, and are either chronically ill or suffer many relapses.

While depression does not lead to schizophrenia, it may arise from it, and may then lead to suicide. Usually it is considered a reaction to the illness, but sometimes it appears to be an intrinsic part of it, when the term schizoaffective may be used.

Drugs — 'major tranquillisers' or neuroleptics — are important in the management of schizophrenia. Funnily enough, the more depressed the person is, the better the outlook.

Dementia

This is the illness most likely to be confused with depression in older people. Complaints of a bad memory are common in depression, and in later life there may be the added fear of 'going senile'. However, many studies have shown that complaining of a bad memory, even in old age, is far more likely to be due to depression than to 'senile dementia'. It can be said, with some confidence:

> "If you're worried about your mind going, then it almost certainly isn't!"

Dementia comes on very gradually, so that it is hard to say just when it started. An episode of depression, on the other hand, can usually be said to have begun in a particular month or even week, or sometimes even on a particular day!

Demented people tend to exaggerate their competence: "Why, I can remember things which happened years and years ago" (which are hard to check!). Depressed people exaggerate their incompetence: "Memory? What memory? I haven't got a memory any more!" If depressed people do badly on memory tests, it is usually because they keep answering "Don't know!" Demented people are usually quite ready to have a go, and then get most of the answers wrong. They get lost even in familiar places, and if they cannot remember something they may even make up a story to fill the gap (confabulate). People who are depressed never do these things.

Demented people tend to be at their worst towards evening (the 'sundown' phenomenon), whereas, of course, the worst time for most depressives is the morning. Unlike most depressives, demented people may be bright and breezy and put a good face on things. Both may sleep poorly and lose weight, but demented people do not lack appetite – they just find it difficult to prepare meals or forget whether they have had them. Dementia tends to get progressively worse, whereas depression nearly always gets better. Depression may, however, result from dementia, especially in the early stages, when there is some awareness that the mind is going.

Alcoholism

This often brings depression in its wake, but it is useless to treat the depression without first confronting the drink problem. While heavy drinking continues, such treatment is almost bound to fail, and is a distraction from the main agenda: alcoholics are frequently keener to excuse their drinking than to stop it. The same goes for drug abuse.

Even when the alcohol abuse is secondary to depression – 'drowning one's sorrows' – it is usually necessary to obtain abstinence before treatment for the depression can be expected to work.

Physical disorders

Cancers and anaemias

These sometimes begin with loss of appetite and weight, and weakness before the physical signs of the disease become obvious.

Parkinson's disease

This causes a mask-like, doleful, inexpressive face and weakness, especially when first getting up. However, the stiffness and shaking of the hands and limbs and the shuffling walk are not really characteristic of depression.

Myxoedema

Myxoedema, the extreme consequence of an underactive thyroid gland, causes a puffy face, a croaky, monotonous voice, and slowness of thought and movement. It develops so gradually that it could be taken for depression by those who see the person nearly every day, whereas those who visit less often will see such a striking change since their last visit that they will be more likely to realise the nature of what is wrong. Myxoedema is treated with thyroid hormone, given very gradually.

Myalgic encephalitis and fatigue syndromes

Myalgic encephalitis (ME) (unkindly nicknamed 'yuppy 'flu') is a state of utter exhaustion associated with muscular pains and tenderness which many believe to follow a special kind of acute viral infection (the exact nature of which is as yet unknown). An early outbreak, in the 1950s, was called 'The Royal Free Disease' because it afflicted a great many nurses at the Royal Free Hospital in Hampstead. Subsequently there was angry argument about whether it was really a strange viral infection or a form of 'mass hysteria' in a close-knit community of young women. The controversy continues, between those who insist that ME is a bodily disorder, so debilitating that it often makes its sufferers depressed, and others who point out that the symptoms and circumstances of the illness are very like a form of depression in which fatigue is to the fore.

It has been argued that the Victorian term neurasthenia, used for a disease of the nervous system causing a state of profound physical and mental fatigue, affecting particularly the professional and educated classes and treated by rest, was essentially the same as the various 'fatigue syndromes' of today, including ME.

As depression and debility can both follow influenza and other virus infections; as many ME sufferers strongly resent any psychiatric label (as if that would mean that their illness was not 'real'), even though there appears to be no treatment for ME except rest and hope; as depression has many physical symptoms and ME many psychological and there are no definite physical signs of ME or depression, the debate is likely to continue. It seems likely, however, that:

(a) not every case of exhaustion that cannot be otherwise explained is due to depression
(b) some cases, however, undoubtedly are
(c) some people can suffer from both
(d) both are real forms of suffering.

9 Treating depression – self, family and others

Self-help is a very important part of treatment, and so is help from family and friends. Support and advice from social services and various voluntary bodies has much to offer. Then there is specialist help, in the form of psychological treatments (including counselling), drugs, electroconvulsive therapy and psychosurgery. Nor should so-called 'fringe' treatments be ignored. This chapter deals with self-help, help from family and friends and social agencies.

Self-help

It has already been said in this book that less than half of those who suffer from depression are likely to have it diagnosed, let alone treated, by a doctor. How do the others manage?

The chances are that most of these undiagnosed depressions are relatively mild and do not last all that

long. This does not mean that they are negligible, but they can usually be weathered – usually without any great disruption of the usual pattern of life. Time (to coin a phrase) is a great healer.

Rudyard Kipling wrote a poem called *How the Camel Got his Hump*. Part of it goes:

"We get the Hump
Cameelious Hump
The Hump that is black and blue!

The cure for this ill is not to sit still
Or frowst with a book by the fire;
But to take a large hoe and a shovel also,
And dig till you gently perspire."

This is excellent counselling. For one thing depressed people are stopped in their tracks by the difficulty in thinking things through, making decisions and doing anything effectively. Physical activity, however, does not make too many demands on the mind, there may be distractions when going for a walk or digging in the garden – a bird, a flower, a building that perhaps was not there before – and the achievement of digging a flower-bed or completing a journey on foot or bicycle helps to off-set negative 'helpless and hopeless' feelings.

'Acting as if' one felt all right, 'carrying on regardless' are also helpful in milder depression. The momentum of a daily routine, particularly if there is a job to go to, helps one to keep going and to continue to do things which may sometimes seem worthwhile. It can be a great comfort when depressed to feel that one has been of some small help to other people. Too demanding a job, however, can lead to overwork in the effort to keep up – working long hours and bringing work home – with increased feelings of inadequacy at not performing properly. Seriously depressed people doubt the good they undoubtedly do, and also doubt their motives:

"Everything I've done has been selfish – not to help others, really, but to make myself feel good."

It is important to eat enough to keep body and soul together, even though one does not much feel like doing so, and the effort of preparing food may seem too much. Wholemeal bread, fresh fruit, vegetables and yoghurt are wholesome, nutritious foods which do not take too much preparation, and they provide calories and vitamins in a pleasant, natural way. Mineral water and fruit juices are also commended. For those who cannot cope with meals, however, highly nutritious soluble powders (like 'Complan' and its successors) are available without prescription from chemists and provide a day's nourishment in concentrated, liquid form.

Alcohol is not forbidden to those who normally enjoy a drink (though care may be needed if an antidepressant has been prescribed — see Chapter 10). However, it is extremely unwise, tempting though it may be to some, to seek to 'drown one's sorrows'. Excessive drinking can aggravate and disinhibit the depression, increasing the risk of suicide, and there is also, of course, the danger of becoming alcoholic.

Everyone, of course, is well advised to stop smoking, but there is no need to do so when one is depressed — a time when one needs all the comfort one can get. Stopping smoking can even precipitate depression in long-term, habitual smokers, although some people lose their taste for tobacco when they are depressed — one of the rare advantages (another is the loss of surplus weight) of the disorder. Strong coffee has a mild stimulant effect, which helps to keep some people going, but may cause unpleasant palpitations and increase insomnia.

For those who cannot sleep it is better to get up, sit in an easy chair and listen to the radio or recorded music, or watch television or a video, than fret, tossing and turning all night; there is a good chance of eventually nodding off in your chair.

Relaxation is helpful, if only it can be achieved. This does not mean staying in bed or collapsing in front of the television like a 'couch potato', but active relaxation: giving time to a relaxation programme as one might to a physical 'work-out'. As has been frequently said already, depression often goes with tension and anxiety, and relaxation can relieve this and give the extra reward of feeling that one is overcoming it oneself: a sense of mastery is a refreshing change for the 'helpless and hopeless' depressed.

Relaxation techniques can be taught (by general practitioners, psychiatrists, psychologists and community nurses) but can also be learnt. Self-help books and leaflets abound, and there are now a number of helpful relaxation tapes (see Appendix 2). These may involve tightening various muscles first, and then relaxing them, usually starting after deep, regular breathing, working up through the body from the feet and toes to the head and neck. Eventually, not only does the body feel thoroughly relaxed, but, by a process of self-hypnosis, the mind is comforted. Obviously it is not a good idea to try this when on one's feet or driving!

A quiet, warm, dark room, comfortable clothing, an easy chair with support for the head, or lying on a bed are ideal. Half an hour devoted to relaxation, once during the day and once before going to sleep, putting away distracting thoughts for that short time, will rest the body and soothe the troubled mind.

Finally, try not to be too British and keep a stiff upper lip! Do cry, if you can. (Many depressed people cannot, but only wish they could.) Do not keep all your feelings to yourself. The research by Professors George Brown and Elaine Murphy has shown how helpful it is to confide. Being able to do so decreases the chance of getting depressed in the first place, and improves the outlook even if one does. On the whole, women are much more able to do this than men, who fear being thought 'wet' or 'wimpish'. But a trouble shared may seem more bearable, even if it is not exactly halved. A lot depends on how one's confidences are received – which leads us into the next section.

Family and friends

"Cheer up, it may not happen
And even though it should
You will not find it half so bad
As now you think it would;
For troubles are but bubbles,
And it may seem rather rum,
But you'll find life's biggest troubles
Are the ones which never come!"

Anyone reciting this cheerful little rhyme to a depressed person would be in danger of being throttled — if depression were not so often accompanied by slowing-up and indecision. Equally unhelpful are "Snap out of it!", "Pull yourself together!", "Stop feeling sorry for yourself!", "Every cloud has a silver lining!", and "Cheer up — you'll soon be dead!"

Many depressed people would like to be less alone in their misery by being able to explain their state to someone with a sympathetic ear. Hasty reassurance or advice are no use to them if they have not been given time to say what they feel, and therefore to believe that they are perhaps half-way understood.

People who interrupt painful disclosures with remarks like:

> "We all feel like that some of the time, you know. You want to think of something cheerful, like where you're going for your summer holidays"

are in effect saying

> "Don't bother me with this! Go away!"

The art of listening is an art, and it is all too rare: one of the ways in which psychiatrists can justify their existence is that they learn how to give their patients a largely uninterrupted hearing for an hour or more, if need be. In ordinary life, however, most people want to turn a 'confession' into a conversation, offering their own experiences and opinions at an early stage. So those who can hold their tongues for a while and let depressed people tell their troubles are certainly friends indeed!

Eventually, of course, something might be said. It will not do to make light of the problem. One would not comfort someone with a broken arm by saying:

> "I'm sure it doesn't hurt as much as you think it does. Anyway, it's your own silly fault. I always said you'd come off that bike sooner or later!"

What might help is:

> "I'm so sorry you've hurt yourself. What bad luck! I bet it was really painful — and it can't be much fun having your arm in a plaster. You won't be able to use it properly for a few weeks, will you? So is there anything I can do to help? Can I drive you to the shops, do the washing for you, etc.? Of course it'll be all right soon after the plaster comes off — though I guess you might need some physiotherapy before you're completely OK."

Such an approach would also do for depression:

> "I'm sorry you feel so wretched, but I'm glad you felt able to tell me about it. I've been told how dreadful it is to suffer from depression, but at least, in the end, it does get better. I understand that there may be treatments which could get you better quicker. You might want to have a word with the doctor. I'd be happy to come along with you and give moral support, if you like – or help in any other way. I could give a hand with the shopping, cooking, sorting out the accounts or looking after the kids, to give you a bit of time to yourself. Please feel free to call on me, if only to off-load, whenever you feel the need."

So, it is particularly helpful to depressed people to:

(a) listen to them more, say less
(b) accept, sympathetically, that they feel bad
(c) remind them that they will get better
(d) point out that medical advice is available
(e) hold back on other advice
(f) offer practical help and support
(g) keep up the support until they are better
(h) keep in touch even if they say that telephone calls and letters make no difference – they do.

Social supports and information

If it is possible to change anything which brought about the depression, then it should be changed. If the dangerous or disabling illness can be cured, the broken relationship restored, employment found for the redundant, debts written off, better housing found, an accountant brought in to complete the baffling tax return – all this is likely to help, though the mood may not lift immediately. To make such changes, help is often needed, because depressed people are too close to their problems to see the 'wood for the trees'. Such help may be forthcoming from family and good friends, or from bodies like the Citizens' Advice Bureau.

For those who belong to a church or other religious group there can be both practical and spiritual support, from the priest or equivalent, and community. Religious doubts may assail the devout (as Bunyan brought out so clearly in *The Pilgrim's Progress*, see Chapter 1), and for them the brotherly or sisterly love and understanding of their fellow-believers can be very valuable, although 'cramming religion down their throats' and making them feel more than ever sinful and backsliding will not. Fortunately many of today's priests, clergymen and rabbis are trained in depression and its management.

Those with major social problems may well see social workers, whose training equips them to help. Not all, however, have much knowledge of depression, and some feel that social factors are paramount, so political action is more important to them than propping up 'the system' by making the best of or 'colluding' (i.e. going along) with it. Social workers attached to general practices and to psychiatric units are usually those best informed about depression.

General practitioners tend to be short of 'talking time', but are often well informed about local helping agencies and can sometimes use their influence, pressing for, say, a change of accommodation on medical grounds. Practice nurses and health visitors may likewise be helpful. Many large practices now employ trained counsellors (see next chapter).

The Samaritans are available anywhere in the country to those who feel desperately depressed, who have only to pick up a telephone to get a patient, uncritical, sympathetic hearing; like psychiatrists, Samaritans are very good at listening. Although the organisation was set up by the Reverend Chad Varah to prevent suicide, you do not have to feel suicidal to call the Samaritans. Samaritans are volunteers – ordinary people who want to help those who are depressed or distressed – but they are carefully screened to eliminate those whose

biases might get in the way of their being sufficiently detached, and they have some training. They are not only available on the telephone, but will actually *see* troubled clients who make their way to their offices. Notorious places for suicide, like Beachy Head and the Clifton suspension bridge, have notices and telephones urging potential suicides to call the Samaritans.

MIND is a charity more for the 'user' of psychiatric services (their preferred term for 'patient') than for psychiatrists. Like the Samaritans, they are greatly 'client-orientated', but they are frequent critics of psychiatry, especially drugs, electroconvulsive therapy, hospital treatment and the 'medical model', but not excepting psychotherapy.

The philosophy of the central (and more political) organisation seems at odds with that of many of its branches, which run day centres for the mentally ill in close collaboration with psychiatric services. Anyway, there is no doubt that MIND cares a great deal about those who suffer 'mental distress', campaigns on their behalf, does its best to advise them, and, at least at a local level, provides practical support.

Relate (the former Marriage Guidance Council) is concerned with those having difficulties in their relationships with their partners and offers a counselling service (not necessarily to bring couples together again, if it appears that they would be better apart).

Depressives Anonymous is an organisation of those subject to and who have weathered depressive illness. CRUSE provides much practical advice as well as support and counselling for widowed people. The Association for Post-Natal Illness is a support group set up by women who have come through post-natal depression, for those who are suffering that disorder. The Manic-Depressive Fellowship (patron: Spike Milligan) is a group of sufferers from that disruptive disorder and those who care for them.

Public libraries are a good source of leaflets and posters drawing attention to a variety of facilities, and the Royal College of Psychiatrists has easy-to-read *'Help is at Hand'* leaflets on *Depression*, *Depression in the Elderly*, and *Bereavement*, as well as other topics which may be related to depression – *Surviving Adolescence*, *Anxiety and Phobias*, *Anorexia and Bulimia* and *Sleep Problems*.

(Further particulars of all these organisations are provided in Appendix 2.)

The media may help too, notably the 'agony aunts' like Virginia Ironside, Clare Rayner and Marjorie Proops, who have personal columns in the newspapers but are besieged with far more problems than they could *ever* publish and have teams of researchers to enable them to give up-to-the-minute authoritative advice and point

You could join 'SELF-PITY ANONYMOUS'...

people in the right direction to get help. Agony aunts are especially useful to shy, lonely people who lack friends and cannot yet face going to see a doctor.

Finally, these days there are a number of telephone 'helplines' which give recorded information. Making a call is expensive, and there is no interaction between the agent and the caller, but the information is usually good.

10 Treating depression – psychological therapies

Psychological therapies are popular with patients because they do not involve taking tablets and appear to make sense. "You're depressed? You have to be depressed about something, so let's find out what it is." "If there's nothing to be depressed about, then just sit down and I'll help you count your blessings." They are also liked because they involve a lot of personal attention: there is no question of feeling 'fobbed off' with a prescription. When the Royal College of Psychiatrists commissioned a nationwide survey of people's attitudes to depression in 1991–92, far and away the favourite treatment was 'counselling'.

The two main forms of psychological treatment are psychotherapy and cognitive therapy. Psychotherapy involves discovering (or 'uncovering') the causes of the depression which the sufferer cannot at present recognise or face. Cognitive therapy deals with the negative feelings which are so often associated with depression, the 'case for the prosecution' which depressed people tend to make against themselves, helping them to take a more charitable and, indeed, positive view.

Despite their attractiveness, these treatments are not in practice easy options. Though very different in theory, they both:

(a) take time
(b) require commitment (by patient and therapist)
(c) require the ability to use words and ideas
(d) are not suitable for severely depressed people (though they may be used when they are somewhat better)
(e) may have to be paid for.

Also, not all depressed people have a sufficiently 'negative self-image' to justify cognitive therapy, nor is there always a 'dynamic formulation' (do not panic, all will be revealed in the next section) to give scope to psychotherapy.

I feel too
DEPRESSED
even to
discuss
my depression...

Psychotherapy

One of Sigmund Freud's greatest achievements was to put the idea of a 'dynamic unconscious' on the map. The unconscious mind is simply everything in our mind of which we are not at this moment conscious, or aware. Some of this is like something in the next room – we only have to go and get it (recall it) to make it conscious. Some is further away, as if in a loft or a cellar – we have to make more effort to remember it, and may need some help (reminders) to find it. Some, however, is locked away, and we do not have the key to the door. It is not just lying around, like lumber, but is active and affects our everyday lives. It is rather like Mr Rochester's poor mad wife in *Jane Eyre*, locked away at the top of a gloomy mansion; Jane is occasionally aware of secret visits to that part of the house, and the odd muffled scream, but cannot fathom the mystery.

The term dynamic refers to the activity of this 'locked away' unconscious, which breaks out in dreams, irrational fears and obsessions, instant likes and dislikes (even falling in love), slips of the tongue, so-called 'Freudian forgetting' (i.e. forgetting what you would rather not remember) and, sometimes, depression. In early life there are supposedly strong feelings and conflicts, especially about parents (once called complexes) which

Shall I go VIA ANGER or VIA GUILT?

are too challenging to be handled at the time, which are 'locked away' by a mental mechanism called repression. However, repressing such fraught material is a bit like dealing with a wound by sticking a bandage over it and then carrying on as if it was not there: it might heal up (leaving a big scar), bleed, fester, or make one unable to walk, or generally unwell.

Similarly, repressed complexes are said to distort the development of the personality, prevent one from achieving one's potential, reduce coping and resilience and cause symptoms of mental illness, especially anxiety and neurosis but also depression.

As has already been mentioned in Chapter 6, there may be a stage in early childhood when a child realises that the 'good' mother who cuddles and feeds him and is loved in return, and the 'bad' mother who is hated for not being around to feed and comfort him, are one and the same being. It used to be said that Freud put everything down to sex, but today the greater taboo is anger. The anger of a little child is overwhelming because he does not know its limits – and he may not even understand whether it comes from within him or from outside. He does not know that he is helpless and harmless – and indeed, if you look at an angry, squalling baby his rage would be terrifying if he were bigger and able to walk.

He could feel that his wrath is a deadly weapon: "I hate you to pieces!", as one of the cartoon cats used to say. But if he destroyed his mother, what would become of him? What terrible reprisals might there not be? Or would he not be all alone, helpless and lost? This is such a huge dilemma for a little person that it is not surprising that it is repressed into the unconscious. (This is a very simplified account of the theories of Melanie Klein, a 'post-Freudian' psychoanalyst, which are particularly appropriate for depression. Like all psychoanalytic theories, it is only a theory — it cannot be proved scientifically. Nevertheless, it provides an approach which seems often helpful in treating depression.)

The effects of this repressed rage (and remorse) could be:

(a) a fear of showing feelings, especially anger
(b) a too careful, cautious, clean, conscientious, 'obsessional' personality
(c) a lack of assertiveness (too much like aggression)
(d) a lack of self-esteem and self-love
(e) a liability to depression in situations which somewhat resemble the original frustrating and frightening dilemma, like conflict at home or work, being deserted, dismissed or the death of a parent.

'Self-love' is not at all the same as selfishness, but very necessary to a fulfilling life. People who boast, or are vain, or seek adoration do not actually love themselves but need reassurance (which can never be enough) that they are lovable, in spite of their huge doubts. (Marilyn Monroe, so beautiful, so clever and so insecure, was a sad example.) Unless one feels basically loved and lovable, it is hard to be loving. "You can't pass on what you never had."

A loving, permissive upbringing which allows emotions (even anger) to be shown but sets reasonable limits on excessive misbehaviour may modify repressed anger and allow it gradually to emerge into consciousness, where it can be recognised as not inevitably destructive but manageable, and accepted. On the other hand, a strict, unemotional (or anyway, undemonstrative) regimented upbringing, with plenty of regulations and penalties, may suppress the 'rage' at the price of its being still active and dangerous.

How can psychotherapy help? It works by bringing these bad feelings back into consciousness and 'disarming' them. This is achieved by the working together (in a 'therapeutic alliance') of the patient (or 'client') and therapist. The simplest situation is 'one to one' — one patient, one therapist, sitting facing each other in a consulting room. The patient tells of the events leading up to this meeting, while the therapist avoids asking more questions than are needed to allow the full story to unfold. If there is a silence the therapist either waits until the patient breaks it, or simply repeats the last word or phrase to encourage the patient to continue. There may, however, be the odd prompt, perhaps suggesting a connection between what has just been said and important happenings in the patient's past, present or future.

The therapist may comment on the patient's behaviour, like being late, lighting a cigarette, sitting on the edge of the chair or raising important issues at the very end of a session, when there is no time to deal with them. Thus the therapist tries not only to help the patient remember more of what may be relevant and important from the past, but also uses the relationship which inevitably develops between patient and therapist as therapy.

This relationship, called transference, has great therapeutic potential. It is called 'transference' because there is a carry-over of feelings about people who were very important in one's early life to the therapist. These feelings may be positive: "I'm so lucky; I've found this wonderful person who is so understanding. She's so clever - and so caring!" (i.e. not unlike the ideal mother!). Or they may be negative: "I can't say I like her. I don't think we're on the same wavelength. The things she says to me are either obvious, downright silly or way out – that is, if she says anything at all. I don't know if I'll go on seeing her – it might be a waste of time. But I really do need help." Oddly enough, it is by calling attention to the negative transference that the therapist is likely to do most good, because while it is easy to admire someone to their face, it is much less easy to be strongly critical.

Some therapists deliberately reveal as little of their real selves as possible, in order to prevent the transference from being limited by any awareness of reality. In psychoanalysis – the lengthiest (going on for years, as in the celebrated case of Woody Allen) and most intense form of psychotherapy – the patient lies on a couch (to better encourage reminiscence and free association, when the patient puts a train of form into words) and the therapist is almost invisible, sitting behind the couch and making an infrequent and brief interpretation.

By interpreting the negative transference the therapist helps to bring feelings of anger, hate, envy and jealousy into the open, where they can be examined and put into proportion. A very important discovery by the patient is that neither the therapist nor the therapy is destroyed by 'letting the anger out'.

It is probably fair to say that psychotherapy is better at solving, or easing, problems in relationships than in lifting the symptoms of depression. The hope is that this will improve the quality of life and reduce the risk of further depression.

Therapy does not have to be carried out on an individual basis. One of the good lessons of World War II was how effective psychotherapy can be for groups of people with similar difficulties, even though personal problems are rarely dealt with in the group, which instead is treated as if it were itself the patient. So the therapist might say, after a patient's outburst, instead of "Jim, perhaps you felt that way because of what Jane was saying earlier about how she felt when her husband was out late and didn't call her?": "Perhaps the group is using Jim to show its anger about my failure to respond to what Jane was telling us about her husband's seeming lack of consideration."

This is a transference interpretation – the therapist is suggesting what the group (not just Jim) may be feeling about him, and why – but it also suggests that Jim is being used to show the anger they may all feel. Group therapy is not simply a dilution of individual therapy, it is a different technique altogether, and sometimes more effective. People like Jim may help to put others in the group in touch with their anger a good deal sooner than may happen in 'one to one' psychotherapy.

I tried an Encounter Group – but I didn't meet anyone...

Similarly, marital therapy treats not two individuals but a mini-group (dyad), the marriage, and family therapy treats not the individual members of the family but the whole family as a sick unit. Dr Robin Skynner interestingly combines marital and group therapy; he and his former patient, the actor John Cleese, have written amusing and instructive books about the process.

There are a bewildering number of schools of psychotherapy – following Freud, Carl Gustav Jung (especially for older people), Klein, Harry Stack Sullivan, Karen Horney, Carl Rogers, R. D. Laing, 'Gestalt' therapy and 'transactional analysis', to name but a few. It cannot be said with confidence that any one is more likely to succeed with depressed people than another – it is a matter of 'horses for courses', the horse being the patient and the course the therapist (as much as the therapy), who are most likely to 'hit it off'.

Lately, especially in the USA, interpersonal therapy (IPT), which is concerned with relationships in the 'here and now' without referring back to the past has been claimed to be as effective as the longer, more probing and uncovering therapies.

How on earth can the troubled patient find the one likely to be of most use? It is difficult enough to find the right general practitioner! However, somehow most of us (at least, those living in the UK) have a general practitioner, who is probably the best person to give such advice. General practitioners might recommend local experts whom they know, psychotherapists attached to the hospitals in which they trained, or those whom they have found to be helpful to other, similar patients.

Guidance is certainly needed: there are as many 'cowboys' among those who claim to be psychotherapists as among so-called plumbers, handymen and builders, and these are given access to one's mind, not just one's property! It is not difficult to imagine how an untrained, irresponsible and unscrupulous 'therapist' might try to exploit a positive transference. Fortunately, measures are being taken to register reputable psychotherapists who have a recognised training and are answerable (as doctors are) to a professional body.

Cognitive therapy

As Freud is to psychoanalysis, so is Dr Aaron Beck, of the University of Pennsylvania, to cognitive therapy. Beck quotes the philosopher Epictetus:

> "Men are disturbed not by things but by the views which they take of them"

and applies this to depression. He describes three patterns of thinking which characterise the depressed person:

(a) his negative view of himself, as defective, inadequate, diseased or deprived — he attributes his unpleasant experiences to this basic defect, and believes that because of this he cannot attain happiness and contentment

(b) he sees the world as making excessive demands on him, and misinterprets his dealings with his environment as representing defeats or deprivation

(c) he has low or no expectations of the future: he expects to fail.

Depressed people deduce the worst, by fastening on a detail rather than a whole experience, using one or two small points to make the worst of everything, exaggerate the bad things and play down the good, wrongly relate external mishaps and disasters to themselves and tend to split their experiences into opposite categories — pure or filthy, perfect or deeply flawed, saint or sinner — always, of course, putting themselves at the worst pole.

Examples of this 'split', 'primitive' thinking and the equivalent 'mature' view, given by Beck are:

Primitive	Mature
I am fearful	I am moderately fearful, quite generous and fairly intelligent
I am a despicable coward	I am more fearful than most people I know
I always have been and always will be a coward	My fears vary from time to time and from situation to situation
I have a defect in my character	I avoid situations too much and have many fears
Since I am basically weak, there is nothing that can be done about it	I can learn ways of facing situations and fighting my fears

Although the 'mature' view admits plenty of problems, it allows far more hope than the 'primitive', which permits none.

Cognitive therapy is much more ordered than psychotherapy and follows a programme personally tailored for the patient. The therapist is more active and the patient is required to be actively engaged too, with homework (recording psychological experiences between sessions, carrying out set tasks). For example, a patient who believes that everyone turns away from him in disgust might be helped to set up a way of judging other people's reactions and then encouraged to assess

their facial expressions and bodily movements in a detached way, with a view to correcting the faulty thinking.

Humour can sometimes be used to help them see the absurdity of some of their notions. (Mel, take a bow!) Basically, patients are required to record their negative ideas and then examine the evidence for and against them. They are also encouraged to return to activities they enjoyed until they became depressed.

Evidence that cognitive therapy works is persuasive. It is as effective as drug treatment in moderately severe depression, and the effects may be more lasting. Combining the two may be the best option. However, cognitive therapy, as has been said, takes time and the therapists are highly trained. It is no work for amateurs but (like psychotherapy) does not have to be carried out by doctors. Professor Isaac Marks, of London's Institute of Psychiatry, has shown that it can be done very successfully by community nurses.

Behaviour therapy

Dogs' mouths water (like ours!) when they smell food. This is a simple reflex. In a series of experiments the great Russian psychologist Pavlov showed that the same reflex can be produced by the bell which means that food is on its way. This is a conditioned reflex. On such a seemingly simple foundation has been built the school of behavioural psychology, with such ill consequences as brain washing and such good as a means of overcoming disabling phobias, and cognitive therapy.

Behaviour therapy usually takes little account of what we think, but concentrates on what we do. Thus fear is a state of having a rapid pulse, tense, shaky limbs, a dry mouth and frequently passing water or even opening the bowels (all of which can be observed and measured), rather than what we actually feel inside. This seems a rather frightening, if not absurd idea to many, but it has been put to good use. A development of Pavlov's ideas by the American psychologist B. F. Skinner uses a powerful tool — operant conditioning. This influences behaviour by only reinforcing what is desired, by in some way rewarding it, while not at all reinforcing what is undesirable (however, not least on ethical grounds, not punishing it).

A neat demonstration of operant conditioning was a trick played on their tutor by a psychology class. When he was lecturing, all those on the left side of the class showed extreme interest in what he was saying, while those on the right showed extreme boredom. He started in the middle of the lecture-room, then drifted to those on the left, who were so responsive to his wit and wisdom. Then halfway through the class the right became extremely interested and the left manifestly bored — whereupon the well-manipulated lecturer switched his attention to the right. They played this game on several occasions, moving him from one side of the room to the other and back!

What has all this got to do with depression? A story from Brice's book, *Psychogeriatrics* (reproduced by permission of Churchill Livingstone, London), will explain:

"Mr Warner became depressed very soon after his retirement. He had never been depressed before. He was extremely agitated, especially in the mornings, when he would literally beat his head against the wall. He would also threaten suicide. His wife started to drink, and she and their five children (though all were living away from home) felt that he should be in hospital. His depression was, indeed, exceptionally severe, and, after several courses of antidepressive drugs, ECT, marital therapy and the offer of a leucotomy (because of his extreme agitation) which he refused, he was no better. He seemed to be stuck in hospital, doomed to become a chronic patient.

However, a 'behavioural modification' programme was devised to discourage 'helpless and hopeless' behaviour and encourage independence. Such basic activities as getting up, dressing, washing, shaving, setting the table and fetching his breakfast were charted every day. The ward staff became interested in his performance, and their interest and approval were among Mr Warner's rewards. Less expectedly, his wife became enthusiastic, joined in and regained some warmth of feeling for him.

In less than a fortnight he was doing everything for himself, and banged his head far less. He helped his less able fellow patients, and was distracted from his gloomy preoccupation with himself while doing so. Soon he was spending days, then week-ends, at home. Not all week-ends were a success, and quite often his wife had to return him to the ward sooner than had been planned. However, she was taught the reward (reinforcement) and discouragement (negative reinforcement) regime by the ward staff, who frequently visited her at home.

Three months after this programme had been started, and after he had been in hospital for a year, he was discharged. With the support of a community psychiatric nurse he attended the Day Hospital every weekday, and regained his interest in woodwork.

He was still nervous, withdrawn, uneasy and liable to frantic despondency, but at times he could really enjoy himself, and he stopped behaving like a sick, fretful child."

The ending of this story is not conventionally happy. After a year at home his wife was fed up with him, and a place was found for him in a residential home, where he settled contentedly enough.

The need for this kind of treatment does not often arise, but it is there for those who do not respond to other methods, especially if they also show very disturbed behaviour.

Counselling

Counselling differs from advice in that it seeks to help people to make their own decisions. Counsellors can take a detached, disinterested (but not unsympathetic or uninterested) view of problems which seem overwhelming and beyond a solution to their clients. They can reassure, restore a sense of proportion and encourage a positive, practical approach. Counselling is more concerned with problem-solving than changing people's personalities. A stalemate in a relationship, whether or not to have an abortion, getting over a bereavement, or some other very upsetting event are all suitable problems for counselling. Compared with psychotherapy, counselling is less concerned with psychodynamics – the unconscious, the past and transference – and concentrates more on the 'here and now'. It involves much more interaction

DEAR DIARY —
Did nothing today —
but no one
noticed..

than traditional psychotherapy, so strained silences are not part of the treatment. It is not so precise and structured as cognitive therapy.

Counselling starts with undivided attention and sympathetic listening, as described in the previous chapter; it goes on to help the client find answers, or if indeed there are no easy answers, to try to accept the inevitable with resignation, fortitude and optimism. It is not endless. A certain number of sessions – say six, or ten – are agreed at the outset, and progress is then reviewed before deciding whether to stop or carry on for a few sessions more.

There are far more counsellors than psychotherapists or cognitive therapists, so most people needing psychological help – especially outside big cities like London – will get it from them. Many general practitioners now have counsellors attached to their practices, but not all are trained. Counsellors need training just as do other psychological therapists, which should include some personal therapy so that they will not let their 'hang-ups' and personal prejudices distort their view of their clients' problems.

11 Treating depression – drugs

A doctor is rarely challenged by patients about prescribing antibiotics: indeed, they will often demand them from him. Few people believe that it is better to 'grin and bear' their headache, strained back, arthritis or bruises without using a painkiller (analgesic): often, indeed, they will beg for one. But there is a strange resistance to taking drugs for depression – so much so that many doctors are quite apologetic if prescribing them.

Why should this be so? The main problem is the confusion between antidepressants and tranquillisers. Tranquillisers (which nearly all belong to the benzodiazepine group of compounds) now have a bad reputation, though they are vastly superior to their predecessors, the sedative barbiturates. They rapidly relieve anxiety (within as little as half an hour), but tend to work less well after being given for a few weeks. Some people become 'tolerant' to them, having to take more and more to get the same effect, and many find them hard to stop because of unpleasant withdrawal symptoms – aching, shaking, hot and cold feelings – which come on within a day or two, or even sooner.

There was a time when general practitioners prescribed tranquillisers all too readily (though in fairness, they were under great pressure from their patients to do so). When the tide turned against these 'pills for personal problems', all sorts of self-help groups were formed to enable people to give up 'tranx' and patients and the public turned against the doctors who had prescribed them and the drug companies which made them, with threats of legal action.

The antidepressants

So patients and their general practitioners became reluctant to use any drugs which affected mood – including the antidepressants. This was throwing a very big baby out with the bathwater. (Oddly enough, benzodiazepines much the same as those used as tranquillisers are still used a lot as sleeping tablets, which people are far more willing to take, even though occasional problems of habituation, tolerance and withdrawal symptoms still apply. Benzodiazepines are also valuable in anaesthesia.)

Before the discovery of the antidepressants in the early 1960s, the drugs given for depression were stimulants or 'pep pills' and could become addictive. They included dexamphetamine ('Dexedrine') and a combination of dexamphetamine and a barbiturate, sodium amytal — 'Drinamyl'. They were useless in severe depression, but 'bucked up' those with milder disorders, and worked almost at once. However, there were nasty 'come downs' as the effects wore off, and if the drug was taken for more than a week or two there was the danger of getting 'hooked'.

The addictive nature of dexamphetamine is shown by its being in demand (as an 'upper') by users of illicit drugs. No antidepressant, on the other hand, has ever been sought by pushers or abusers: why?

(a) Antidepressants take far too long to work: no one needing a quick 'fix' can wait a month or more for the effects.

(b) They are not stimulants. They do nothing for those who are not depressed — except give them side-effects!
(c) They simply restore to normal the mood of a number (more than half) of those who are depressed.

When, which and for how long?

If antidepressants take so long to work, there is no point in giving one to someone whose depression is likely to clear up in a week or two. So (unless it is very severe) it would be best to wait for two or three weeks, in case it goes away.

If the depression is relatively mild, firstly the cure with antidepressants could be worse than the disease, as they all have some side-effects. Secondly, the antidepressant might not work all that well anyway. Professor Gene Paykel of Cambridge, using a measure of depressive symptoms called the Hamilton Depression Rating Scale has shown that those with a score of less than 12 do no better on antidepressant than on placebo, while those with a higher score do much better on the drug.

People who do not like the idea of taking tablets should be allowed not to do so (there is not much choice, anyway!) but should be given the chance to change their mind if the depression gets worse or their preferred method of treatment is not working. Some psychotherapists discourage the use of tablets while patients are in therapy, seeing it as 'hedging bets' or a distraction from the main agenda. Others, though, permit drugs for those who are quite severely depressed, though they may not wish, or be qualified, to prescribe them themselves.

People who have been depressed before and who have responded to a particular antidepressant should go back on it at the first sign of relapse.

Very severely depressed people, who are actively suicidal or have stopped eating and drinking or are deluded, are unfit for treatment with antidepressants at home and need to be in hospital and, probably, need electroconvulsive therapy (see next chapter).

Generally, then, antidepressants are considered for those who have been at least moderately depressed for at least two weeks, whose depression is more than just a mild reaction to events (e.g. when the charge of shoplifting is dropped instead of being relieved they say "But I need to be punished!"), if the symptoms are typical of depression (waking early, worse at the beginning of the day, appetite and weight loss, no joy, etc.) and, of course, if the patient is willing to take them.

Which antidepressant depends to some extent on which the doctor knows – there are so many. Most

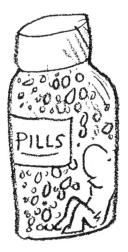

doctors prescribe one or two drugs they have got to know pretty well. However, it would be usual to start with a tricyclic (see pp. 80—83) and then, if it did not work or there were uncomfortable side-effects, to try something else with a different way of working or with fewer or different side-effects.

If antidepressants do not work the main reason is that patients do not take them! This question of compliance is exceedingly important. People may not comply because:

(a) they feel 'fobbed off' with a prescription when they want to talk about their troubles
(b) they do not understand what the drug is supposed to do, and expect to feel better at once
(c) they are afraid of the side-effects, or dislike those they do experience ("I took your tablets for a day, and I couldn't stand up straight!")
(d) their families or friends put them off: "I wouldn't take those if I were you — my friend was on nerve tablets and they made her hands shake, and she couldn't keep still, and she had to see a psychiatrist. Why don't you see my aromatherapist instead?"
(e) the dose of the antidepressant is inadequate — enough to cause some side-effects but too little to lift the mood.

One thing is certain, you cannot be helped by a drug you have not taken: "Mrs Jones didn't respond to not taking 'Tofranil' — let's see how she gets on with not taking 'Prozac'!"

It seems that (a) explaining the treatment and (b) keeping in touch during the early days, are rather more important in ensuring good compliance than the particular drug prescribed.

How long? The present evidence is that effective treatment should be continued for six months after recovery in younger people, and perhaps for two years in older, to reduce the risk of relapse.

How much? Giving the lowest dose (as general practitioners tend to do) is less effective than the full dose, which is twice as much, side-effects permitting.

The monoamine oxidase inhibitors (MAOIs)

Although these are not much used now, they were the first antidepressants to be discovered, so will be discussed first. Iproniazid, a drug used to treat tuberculosis, was noticed, by a happy accident, to lift depression in depressed tuberculous patients. Although too toxic (to the liver) to be used safely enough, similar but safer drugs were developed, and so the defeat of depression by drugs began.

How do they work? The neurotransmitter theory of depression is discussed in Chapter 6 (see neurotransmitters, pp. 37–38). Messages are transmitted from one nerve cell to another by the passage across the tiny gap between the nerve endings (synapse) of a chemical produced by the cell which is sending the message. These chemicals, called neurotransmitters, belong to the class of compounds known as monoamines, and they are thought to be deficient in depression. All the antidepressants seem to work by, in their different ways, increasing the amount of neurotransmitter available in the synapse.

Normally, once the monoamine messenger has stimulated the receptors of the next cell, it is removed from the synapse. One way of doing this is by the release of a substance called an enzyme which makes the neurotransmitter inactive. All enzymes end in '-ase'. Those which act on the neurotransmitters are called monoamine oxidases – that is 'the enzyme which inactivates the neurotransmitter by combining it with oxygen (oxidation)'. What the MAOIs do is to prevent this enzyme from working – they inhibit it. So the monoamine stays in the synapse longer, and this helps to lift the depression.

That, as it were, is the good news. The bad is that MAOIs do not just act in the synapses in the brain but they affect processes in other parts of the body. The most important of these actions is on foods and drink rich in an amino acid called tyramine. MAOIs prevent tyramine from being broken down in the normal way, and the result can be a rapid rise in blood pressure and a violent throbbing headache at the back of the head. At best this is extremely unpleasant, at worst there can be a fatal stroke. Tyramine is in pickled herrings, caviare, broad bean pods, meat and yeast extracts like 'Bovril', 'Oxo' and 'Marmite', Chianti wine, and cheese: the tyramine reaction is often referred to as the 'cheese reaction'. People on MAOIs have to avoid all these foods, go easy on the alcohol, and also avoid certain medicines (some of which can be bought over the counter, like cough and cold cures). An MAOI card is given with the prescription as a reminder of these precautions.

All this sounds pretty terrifying, yet depression can be much more so, and MAOIs, though never the first choice in treatment, sometimes work where other antidepressants do not. It is not difficult to avoid the banned foods and medicines in practice and (if the worst comes to the worst) there is an antidote, although only a well equipped general practitioner or a casualty department would have it.

The MAOIs include isocarboxazid ('Marplan'), phenelzine ('Nardil') and tranylcypromine ('Parnate'). All are given as one or two tablets up to three times a day. 'Parnate' is the most powerful (and the most likely to cause the 'cheese reaction'); unlike almost every other antidepressant, it sometimes acts within a week. All, but especially 'Parnate', can cause a sharp drop in blood pressure when standing up after sitting or lying down ('orthostatic hypotension'), which means faintness or even passing out. So a warning has to be given not to leap up or charge upstairs, but to take things easy and get up slowly. 'Parnate' may also make it hard to get off to sleep if taken after 2 p.m.

RIMAs may be giving the MAOIs a new lease of life. The letters stand for 'reversible inhibitors of monoamine oxidase subtype A'. There are two important monoamine oxidase inhibitors, types A and B, and it is B which, when inhibited, gives rise to the 'cheese reaction'. As RIMAs act only on type A, the usual dietary precautions are less strict. Also their action wears off after a day, rather than a fortnight as is the case with the older MAOIs. The first RIMA to be introduced to the UK is moclobomide ('Manerix'). It may be no more effective than its predecessors, but safer.

The monoamine reuptake inhibitors (MARIs)

Another way of removing the neurotransmitter from the synapse is by 'reuptake' (an active form of reabsorption) by the nerve cell which released it in the first place. MARIs (monoamine reuptake inhibitors) act by blocking or slowing down this reuptake, so increasing the availability of the neurotransmitter at the synapse. MAOIs stop it being broken down; MARIs stop it being reabsorbed.

Three forms of MARIs will be discussed — the old tricyclics, the new tricyclics and the serotonin reuptake inhibitors.

The old tricyclics

Tricyclics (so-called, in case any chemists among our readers are interested, because the molecule contains three linked six-sided rings, with a side-chain) were discovered very soon after the MAOIs, in 1956. The first, imipramine, was introduced for the treatment of schizophrenia, and did not work. However, it helped depression instead — another happy accident.

The oldest are imipramine and amitriptyline. Imipramine ('Tofranil') is a strong antidepressant with possible anticholinergic side-effects (reducing the activity of another neurotransmitter, acetyl choline) which include:

  a dry mouth
  blurring of vision
  difficulty in passing water (especially, but not
      exclusively, in men)

constipation

sweating

difficulty in getting an erection and ejaculating (or in 'getting it up' and 'coming' – not all that important to the deeply depressed, but of more consequence to those who are getting better).

Other side-effects include:

a drop in blood pressure on standing, which can result in falling

weight gain, especially when the treatment is established

effects on the heart, sometimes causing an irregular pulse and heart-block, but not often of any consequence

rarely, fits, especially in those inclined to epilepsy.

There may also be interactions with other drugs. The interaction may either make one or other drug no longer effective, or be dangerous (e.g. with the MAOIs). Some drugs for blood pressure, stomach ulcers, antihistamines (given for hay fever) and the contraceptive pill may all affect or be affected by tricyclics. In practice, though, these interactions are not often much of a problem.

We know that imipramine works because, like most other antidepressants, it has been tested against placebo in a double-blind trial. That means that patients suffering from depression have been randomly divided into a group which gets the drug and a group which gets a 'dummy', which looks just the same but in fact contains no drug at all. 'Double-blind' means that neither the patients in the trial nor those who are assessing them know whether they are getting the drug or the placebo until the trial is over.

Such studies, essential to demonstrate the value of any new treatment (and some old, which may owe more to tradition and faith than to science) show that depressed people do decidedly better on imipramine than do those on placebo, and that this is highly unlikely to be due to chance. Such trials also look at adverse reactions, which are always found to some extent in the placebo group (the idea of being on a new drug brings fears as well as hopes), so learning which should be attributed to the drug and how endurable they are.

Imipramine is an 'energising' antidepressant, and not very sedative; indeed, it may cause increase in agitation in those who are already inclined that way. Amitriptyline ('Tryptizol'), for many years the most widely prescribed antidepressant, on the other hand, is sedative, which is a good thing in those who are agitated and cannot sleep but may cause drowsiness by day (as well as all the other side-effects mentioned about imipramine) so that accidents may happen and warnings must be given against driving and using machinery. Some patients, however depressed, feel so like 'zombies' on these older tricyclics that they simply cannot go on taking them.

Two further snags of these tablets are the long time they take to work and their dangerousness in overdosage.

Seriously depressed people are potentially suicidal, and may use impulsively whatever means may be to hand — which could be the tablets they have been prescribed for their depression. Tablets differ a lot in how dangerous they are in overdosage. Benzodiazepines, for instance, are pretty safe, whereas nearly all antidepressants are possibly dangerous. So in the early stages of treatment not too many tablets should be issued at a time, or they should be given into someone else's safe-keeping. Most importantly, the prescribing doctor should see the patient frequently at the beginning of treatment, to give advice, support and encouragement, and not just hand over a month's supply saying "Come back when you've finished those!"

Imipramine and amitriptyline are given up to three times a day. They are very cheap to the National Health Service.

Clomipramine ('Anafranil') is a powerful antidepressant with all the side-effects of imipramine only more so. It acts mainly on the neurotransmitter serotonin (of which more, later). It is not a first choice in the treatment of depression, but is one of those brought in if the first choice does not work. 'Anafranil' also helps in obsessional and phobic disorders.

Dothiepin ('Prothiaden') is a useful tricyclic, less activating than imipramine, less sedative than amitriptyline, with fewer and less severe side-effects than either and therefore better tolerated by patients – that is they are more likely to take it! It is usually given at night, and may help with sleep from the time when it is started; the once-a-day dosage helps those who find it difficult to remember when to take their tablets. Another advantage is that 'Prothiaden' (like 'Tryptizol', and most of the sedative tricyclics, but not at all like imipramine or clomipramine) can be safely combined with an MAOI if need be (see below).

Other older tricyclics (which are simply listed here) are:

protryptyline ('Concordin')
doxepin ('Sinequan')
trimipramine ('Surmontil')
nortryptyline ('Aventyl') and
desipramine ('Pertofran').

The newer tricyclics

These are supposed to have fewer side-effects but to be just as effective as the older. Here are some examples.

Lofepramine ('Gamanil'), two or three times a day, is usually very well tolerated, and is said to be relatively safe if an overdose is taken.

Trazodone ('Molipaxin'), taken by day after meals or in a single dose at night, is one of the more sedative newer drugs, but with hardly any cholinergic side-effects. Rarely it causes priapism, a permanent erection, which is much less fun than it sounds!

Sort-of tricyclics

Maprotiline ('Ludiomil') is a tetracyclic – that is, it has four of those six-sided rings in its molecule instead of three. However, it acts very much like a newer tricyclic.

Mianserin ('Bolvidon') is a mild, rather sedative antidepressant, with few other side-effects, but has been used rather less since it was found occasionally to have serious effects upon the bone marrow.

The serotonin-specific reuptake inhibitors (SSRIs)

The tricyclics act, to a greater or lesser extent, on two main neurotransmitters, noradrenaline and serotonin. Evidence that serotonin (also known as 5-hydroxytryptamine, or 5-HT) is particularly important in depression (and suicide) is growing. Recently drugs have been developed which increase the amount of serotonin at the synapses without affecting noradrenaline – they are serotonin-specific.

There are now four SSRIs (and likely soon to be more): fluvoxamine ('Faverin'), sertraline ('Lustral'), fluoxetine ('Prozac'), and paroxetine ('Seroxat'). While they have far fewer anticholinergic side-effects than the tricyclics, they are more likely to cause nausea and indigestion, so it is recommended that they are not taken on an empty stomach. They are less likely than other antidepressants to cause a gain in weight – indeed, 'Prozac' can be used in bulimia.

One or other of the SSRIs will undoubtedly suit some patients who cannot tolerate the tricyclics, especially those who feel over-sedated (or 'zombie-like') on less than therapeutic doses. However, 'new' does not always mean better, and some patients will not be able to endure the nausea they may feel when they first take SSRIs. Individuals may benefit more from SSRIs than the older drugs, and the choice now available to patients and doctors has been increased, but, overall, the evidence that they are more effective is lacking.

They are also, at present, quite expensive – which matters to cost-conscious health authorities, insisting on 'value for money'! The counter-argument is that drugs which are actually taken and get people better are better value than those which are not and do not. Doses are mostly just once a day.

Other antidepressants

L-tryptophan ('Pacitron', 'Optimax'), an amino-acid in the diet, is turned by the body into serotonin. It also gets to the nerve-endings in the brain, providing more fuel, as it were, for the manufacture of serotonin there, for release into the synapse. In its own right it is a pretty weak antidepressant, and might as well be regarded as a foodstuff (rather like a vitamin) than as a drug. It works best as a boost to other antidepressants, such as the MAOIs or lithium. After decades of safe use it was recently withdrawn following a scare in the USA, but it is hoped that it will soon be returned to general use. Two to four pretty large tablets are taken, up to three times a day ("almost a meal in themselves!" some patients have been known to say).

Flupenthixol ('Fluanxol') has a mildly stimulating action, within a few days, which justifies its occasional use in the treatment of mild depression. One or two tablets are given twice a day, and can act within a week.

Caffeine, in coffee and tea, lifts the mood, which is why we drink those beverages. Too much coffee, however, causes sleeplessness and palpitations.

Lithium and the mood regulators

Lithium is a very close cousin to sodium, which is in common salt, baking powder and all the cells and fluids of the body. If given as a simple compound, lithium carbonate, it displaces some of this body sodium, and thus gets into the cells. So what has this to do with treating depression? The truth is that there are so many effects on the body and the brain that we do not quite know which are relevant.

Are any? What is the evidence that lithium works? Its first use on psychiatric patients was by Dr Cade in Australia. In 1949 he noted that guinea pigs injected with lithium did not react to stimulants, but they did not become sleepy either. Then he gave lithium to violent psychiatric patients, and found that it calmed those who were manic.

Later the Norwegian Professor Mogens Schou found that giving lithium to people with manic–depression who kept relapsing sometimes stopped these relapses or made them shorter and less severe, with longer intervals between them. For some reason this treatment did not catch on for some years. The difference between the dose of lithium needed to stabilise the mood and that which is quite toxic is small. As this risk – of causing shaking, weakness, diarrhoea, vomiting and delirium – was plain, while the benefits of lithium were not seen for a year or two, many doctors were not convinced that the treatment was worthwhile. In recent years, however, lithium has surged back into favour, in view of the overwhelming evidence that it works. Not only does it prevent or reduce relapse (in 'unipolar', or 'never manic' as well as 'bipolar' illness), but it also enhances the action of antidepressants. So successful has it been that the need for electroconvulsive therapy (next chapter) has been reduced.

Too little lithium is useless; too much toxic. This is true, of course, of almost any drug, but in the case of lithium the difference between the two is quite small, and varies a great deal from one person to another. Consequently it is necessary to check the level by taking blood: at first this is done every week until the dose is right, then every month for three months, then every three to six months to check that it is still at the right level — for years. A change to a hot climate, an attack of diarrhoea and vomiting, being put on a diuretic drug (to increase the amount of water passed) — all may alter the lithium requirements and so extra blood tests must be done urgently.

Side-effects may include a fine tremor of the hands, dry mouth with a 'metal' taste, tiredness and passing a lot of water. Later side-effects include weight gain (the curse of so many drug treatments for depression) which may sometimes be because lithium can suppress the action of the thyroid gland: the answer is to check the thyroid's activity every six months, and if it is underactive either stop the lithium or give thyroid hormone (thyroxine). Another occasional late side-effect is passing huge amounts of water with a thirst to match because of the effects of lithium on the kidney (known as 'nephrogenic diabetes insipidus'). This usually clears up if the lithium is stopped.

These side-effects are serious, but most people who need to can take lithium for years without problems. Even where there are problems the patient may think the benefits of treatment outweigh them.

> Mrs C, in her 70s, had suffered manic depression ever since she gave birth to her daughter at the age of 27. She quite enjoyed her mildly manic spells, when she would go on a spending spree, but the depressions were hell: fortunately they would lift after up to six treatments of electroconvulsive therapy (ECT). But now the ECT no longer worked and she was spending nine months in the year depressed. She suffered from heart failure from time to time, and had only one kidney. Nevertheless, her life was so wretched that lithium was tried: it worked wonderfully well! She then spent her life in a happy state of equilibrium. Although, on two occasions she suffered episodes of lithium toxicity, she recovered quickly and insisted that she wanted to continue the

treatment. At 85 she developed cancer. She coped bravely, though she knew the outcome. In her last days she whispered to her daughter: "I'm so glad I'm not dying depressed!"

Unfortunately about half those who have been well while taking it relapse within six months of stopping it.

Mrs M, in her 60s, had a long history of manic and depressive bouts, admissions to psychiatric hospitals and suicide attempts. She was put on lithium and settled down. She was pretty well, with only the mildest mood swings, for five years but wanted to do without the lithium because she was putting on weight. Within a week she was high: "at last you're seeing the real me!" She was boisterous, overactive, told her husband, daughters and doctors off, and refused to go back on the lithium: "It's been holding me back for years!" Two months later she swung into a state of agitated depression with strong suicidal impulses. She was given a tranquilliser (lorazepam) for her agitation, an SSRI antidepressant (paroxetine) for the depression and lithium was resumed. Readmission was narrowly avoided. Within two months she was back to her former state and has remained so ever since. She is now adamant that she would never want to try without lithium again.

Pregnancy presents special problems. Lithium can damage the baby in the womb (foetus) in the early weeks, so women who are taking lithium ought to stop it if they want to conceive, but stopping lithium for that reason carries quite a risk of relapse. The lithium can be resumed after three months of pregnancy, but requirements will alter as the pregnancy goes on and especially at the time of birth, so the levels have to be watched very closely. Women with bipolar illness are at great risk of relapse after they have given birth, so the lithium must be maintained, even though the baby cannot be breast fed because lithium comes through in the breast milk. (Incidentally, there is little or no evidence that other antidepressants damage the foetus or appear in the breast milk.)

Carbamazepine ('Tegretol') is a fascinating drug. It is an anti-epileptic, a specific treatment for neuralgia, can be used for diabetes insipidus (one of the causes of which is lithium therapy, see above) and it can be used, either with or instead of lithium, as a mood regulator. It is a weaker regulator than lithium, but safer (especially for those with heart and kidney problems) and there is no need for blood tests. It may be especially useful for 'rapid cycling', that is where there are four or more bouts of depression or mania in a year.

Other anti-epileptic drugs have an occasional place as second- or third-choice mood regulators (e.g. 'Valproate').

This has been a long chapter. It shows that there is a lot more to the underrated drug treatment of depression than just handing out a few tablets. How do doctors find their way through so many choices?

(a) Having decided that the depression is at least moderately severe and unlikely to go away soon, they prescribe one of the more easily tolerated tricyclics, like dothiepin or lofepramine, after fully explaining the effects and possible side-effects.

(b) They review the treatment after a week or two to check that the pills are being taken, to note any side-effects, answer any questions and encourage persistence if there are problems; usually, however, there are not.

(c) In three or four weeks, if the depression has lifted, they keep the patient on that dose for at least six months, and wean them slowly off the drug.

(d) If the depression has not lifted, they increase the dose to the maximum for another two to three weeks.

(e) If there is no response they check once again that the pills are being taken, then seek the help of a psychiatrist and try:

funny—
I thought I just came from there...

DEPRESSION

(i) a stronger tricyclic, like clomipramine
(ii) an MAOI, like phenelzine
(iii) an SSRI, like fluoxetine
   for another month.

(f) If the depression lifts, they continue as under (c).
(g) If not, they might try another drug under (e), but they would have to wait two weeks after stopping an MAOI before they could try either of the others, and six weeks after stopping fluoxetine before they could try an MAOI. Or they could:

(i) combine the MAOI with one of the more sedative tricyclics (e.g. dothiepin, amitriptyline, trimipramine)

(ii) add L-tryptophan (if available)
(iii) add lithium carbonate (which would be used earlier for manic–depression)
(iv) add thyroid hormone, which very occasionally helps 'refractory' depression.

(h) If none of the above work, or if the patient is very agitated, deluded, suicidal or not eating or drinking, the psychiatrist will almost certainly

(i) consider admitting the patient to a psychiatric ward
(ii) suggest electroconvulsive therapy.

Electroconvulsive therapy is the subject of the next chapter.

12 Treating depression — physical treatments

Electroconvulsive therapy (ECT)

Surgeons do the most astonishing things to people's bodies. Not too long ago, the more robust had a philosophy: "When in doubt, cut it out!" and would hack merrily away, with their patients' and society's approval, even when the benefits were not always obvious, nor the patient's survival guaranteed.

Psychiatrists have one 'physical' treatment, exceedingly safe, leaving no scars and used only after careful consideration, to relieve people in an extremity of misery and it works — yet they are damned for it! Nothing stigmatises psychiatry more, not even the Gothic asylums they inherited from the last century, than its endorsement of electroconvulsive therapy (ECT).

Anthony Clare observes (in the book he wrote with Spike Milligan) (see Appendix 2):

"I am often asked whether I give ECT. When I answer that I do if there are clinical indications, I invariably encounter a hostile response, a reaction that suggests that I am some kind of Frankenstein, a fiendish Caligari blowing the minds of my helpless patients when I can think of nothing better to do. People who regard themselves as rational observers of the human condition and open to reasoned argument go glazed around the eyes and their expression adopts that closed, intolerant look. Nothing I can say can change their minds. They know that ECT is barbarous. After all, does it not consist of shocking, jolting, electrocuting the brain?"

So, what is the truth? Chapter 7 — What is the outlook? — describes how things were before the discovery of ECT (by chance) in 1938 (when, as Dr William Sargant used to say, there was all the time in the world for psychological treatments, because that was all they had!). Cerletti and Bini in Rome had the idea that schizophrenia and epilepsy were incompatible – one could not exist with the other; so they gave schizophrenic patients fits by injecting them with camphor. Their theory was quite wrong – people with epilepsy are rather more likely to develop schizophrenia than other people – and the fits did little for the unfortunate schizophrenics in their care. However, they had a most dramatic effect on the long-term melancholic patients who came suddenly out of their depressive stupor. Cerletti and Bini concluded, rightly, that it was the fit or convulsion which wrought this miracle, and they set about finding a more precise and humane way of inducing a fit than the camphor injections. The answer was to do it by passing an electric current across the brain for a split second.

This treatment used to be given 'straight', that is without anaesthesia. Those who have seen the films *The Snake Pit* or *One Flew Over the Cuckoo's Nest* will know how it was done.

The patient was held down by about six people, a gag was placed in the mouth (to avoid damage to the tongue and teeth) the electrodes were applied to the temples and the current was passed by turning a handle or pressing a button. The patient at once lost consciousness and had a fit – a great spasm of the body's muscles, then violent jerking movements for a minute or so – followed by a deep sleep, and waking within half an hour, sometimes feeling achy or muzzy for a while, but recovering fully within an hour. Those who remember with disgust Jack Nicholson's treatment in *One Flew Over the Cuckoo's Nest* rarely remember that he was completely unaffected by the ordeal, and was teasing the awful 'Nurse Ratched' as soon as he returned to the ward!

However, 'straight' ECT was unpleasant for those who gave it and not without risk to limb, though rarely to life: occasionally an arm was broken or a vertebra crushed. In the 1960s, modified ECT was introduced: the treatment was modified by a short-acting anaesthetic and a muscle relaxant, so that when the current is passed, the fit is largely confined to twitching of the toes – very undramatic, though a full fit as far as the brain, if not the body, is concerned. Modified ECT is a little riskier than 'straight' because an anaesthetic is given, but it is still exceedingly safe.

Most patients who require ECT at all require a course of six to ten treatments, or possibly more, given twice or three times a week. In patients suitably selected, that is suffering from severe depression, the treatment succeeds for eight out of ten.

There are so many misapprehensions about ECT that we will list the main ones and try to deal with them.

ECT is a shock treatment

It is not, it is a way of producing fits. It has nothing to do with the cruel attempts in past ages to scare or beat patients back into their senses.

It is a form of punishment

No, to use it that way is an abuse. It was used as a punishment in *One Flew Over the Cuckoo's Nest*, but that was an allegory, not a documentary. Certainly ECT has been abused in the past, but this is now quite inappropriate and unethical.

It works — if it works at all — by wiping out the memory

Some memory loss is an occasional, undesired side-effect of ECT. It is not necessary if the treatment is to be effective, it is unwanted, and attempts have been made to reduce it by keeping the voltage as low as possible or placing the electrodes on the non-dominant side of the head (which is usually the side on which we are handed — right or left). Actually far more patients find their memory improved by ECT (because it lifts the depression which makes the memory bad) rather than even temporarily impaired.

You do not really know how it works

No, we do not exactly know how ECT works — just as we do not know quite how lithium works, or did not until fairly recently know how aspirin works — but we do know that it does work, and that it is the fit, and not the electricity, that is needed. Experiments have been made comparing ECT with 'ET' (electrotherapy) — just putting the patient to sleep and passing a current through the head too weak to cause a fit — and then having the results judged by someone who does not know who had which treatment. If the depression is severe, ECT is far better.

The effects do not last

Having had ECT is no guarantee that it will never be needed again. Indeed, severe depression puts one at risk of further severe depression later in life. But ECT is very likely to cure this episode of depression. Very few medical treatments, unlike surgical, guarantee that the illness will not happen again – asthma, diabetes, gout, pneumonia can all be treated now, but are likely to recur.

It causes permanent damage to the brain

No, this is a myth. Patients who complain of memory problems long after ECT are in fact highly likely to be suffering from residual depression, of which memory impairment is, of course, a symptom.

ECT does not solve the problems which caused the depression

True, but it puts the patient in a state where those problems can be faced and, perhaps, tackled.

ECT is given to helpless patients against their will

The patient's written consent is needed to this as to any other treatment. Neither the psychiatrist nor the anaesthetist could legally go ahead without it. The only exception is for desperately ill patients – suicidal, not eating or drinking, deluded about being too wicked or in imminent danger of death – who can be compelled

to have ECT if they are first placed on a Treatment Order under the Mental Health Act 1983 (which involves an independent social worker and the general practitioner as well as the psychiatrist) and then an independent psychiatrist nominated by the Mental Health Act Commission (i.e. not one of the psychiatrist's mates) agrees that the treatment is necessary and that up to a specified number of treatments may be given: the precautions are quite remarkable! (These are the arrangements in England and Wales, but much the same apply in most other countries.)

Psychiatrists are sadistic, unhinged, power-mad agents of a corrupt regime who get their kicks...

Ah! Well, of course, now you're talking!

Psychosurgery

All the bad feelings in the public's mind about ECT are magnified several times when it comes to lobotomy, leucotomy or what is now called psychosurgery. The old operations, pioneered in the 1930s, severed the links between the very front and the rest of the brain and thereby 'cut the worry nerve'. They produced some spectacular improvements in patients showing 'tortured self-concern', at the cost of not uncommon personality change (towards a much more callous, coarse, self-centred person) and a liability to fits; occasionally, of course, there were deaths.

The procedure was grossly overused in many mental hospitals in the USA and the UK, especially for schizophrenic patients, and it fell into disrepute when modern treatments, especially the neuroleptic, antidepressant and tranquillising drugs, came on line in the 1960s.

However, the operation has been considerably refined. Instead of cutting nerve fibres, radioactive seeds with a short half-life are placed in exactly the right part of the brain with a needle, using a highly sophisticated technique called stereotaxis. Psychosurgery by this method has very few of the snags and all the advantages of the old operation.

So who needs it nowadays? Well, there are still a few very agitated people, suffering from severe depression, obsessional—compulsive or anxiety states, for whom all other treatments have ultimately failed, and for whom psychosurgery offers the only respite from a living hell which is quite likely to drive them to suicide. It is easy to dismiss psychosurgery, as further evidence of the psychiatrist as Frankenstein, when one has been fortunate enough never to meet anyone in this extreme state of suffering.

Because of the bad public image of psychosurgery, the precautions in the Mental Health Act of 1983 in England and Wales against its abuse are astonishing. Not only can it never be performed against the patient's will, but even if patients beg for it they cannot have it unless three Mental Health Act Commissioners are satisfied that they are in a fit state to know what they are letting themselves in for. There is the danger of a 'catch 22' situation here – a truly ill, desperate patient could be deemed too distraught to make a balanced decision about what is actually needed. Nevertheless, despite these unique safeguards, about 30 people in England and Wales have this 'last resort' treatment every year.

Arguably the world's greatest authority on psychosurgery is Dr Paul Bridges, of the Brook Hospital, London. Almost all the candidates for psychosurgery in this country are referred to him at the Geoffrey Knight Neurosurgical Unit. His experience is that most of these patients have been inadequately treated with antidepressants, and that most can still be helped with medication; only a minority actually need psychosurgery. But for those who need it, it is a godsend.

13 Treating depression – the fringe and beyond

Sleep

Surely it makes good sense for the stressed and weary depressed patient to be treated with rest and sleep? On admission to a psychiatric ward the patient naturally expects to go to bed and be nursed there – and may be disagreeably surprised to find that bed is very much for night-time and patients are expected to be up and about, attending ward meetings and occupational therapy, and sharing ward chores.

There was a vogue for 'narcosis therapy' going back at least until the American Civil War, when it was used for combat-weary soldiers, but it has fallen into disrepute. One reason is that the benefits did not last for very long. The 'sleeping beauty' would wake, refreshed, from her long lie-in, but there was no 'Prince Charming' and after a week or two old problems would crowd in. The other reason is that it is not at all easy to keep people asleep for most of the day, for weeks on end,

without their becoming over-sedated, with risks of bed-sores, dehydration, falls and even pneumonia. There are still ripples from the scandal of a private hospital in Australia, where several deaths from the complications of narcosis were covered up, and the previously honoured director took his life before he could be brought to account for them.

In fact, far from putting depressed patients to sleep, there are better grounds for keeping them awake! Sleep-deprivation can dispel depression, but it is hard to continue and when sleep returns to normal the depression is likely to return too. It is sleep in the second half of the night which needs to be stopped – say from 2 a.m. or 3 a.m. onwards. Depression is typically worse straight after waking, not only in the morning but sometimes after a nap during the day, which suggests some connection between sleep before waking, and depression.

Hypnosis

The technical term for a sleeping tablet is an hypnotic, but hypnosis does not involve actually putting people to sleep. Instead it puts them into a trance in which they can forget what the hypnotist has asked them to do but will still do it, at the right time and in the right place, according to the hypnotist's instructions: this is one of the neatest demonstrations of the working of an unconscious mind. But can this be used to help the person who is depressed? Not really.

Hypnosis can be used to explore the unconscious, but the results are not as good as those obtained by conventional psychotherapy – perhaps because the subject feels less able to 'own' material brought to light by these 'magical' means. Freud gave up hypnosis early in his career (although some say that was because he was not much of a hypnotist). Hypnosis does not lift depression, and the effects of suggesting to subjects that they now feel happy are shallow and transitory at best. However, hypnosis can be used as an aid to relaxation (see Chapter 8 – What is not depression?).

Light

Most of us find our spirits rising in the spring, as the daffodils, crocuses and snowdrops appear and the days are longer. Many depressed people, however, do not react this way and feel at their worst in the spring, which is a peak season for suicide. But those who suffer seasonal affective disorder (SAD; Chapter 3 – How common is depression?) look forward keenly to this time of the year, when their mood is likely to lift.

Artificial light has been found to help SAD: it has to be bright, four hours a day is best, and, surprisingly, the effects depend on seeing the light, not basking in it. It works in a week or so, and wears off very quickly out of the light. It may have some effect on serotonin levels.

'Mens sana in corpore sano'

'A healthy mind in a healthy body' is a sensible approach to life, and advice about exercise and a balanced diet has been given in Chapter 8. Cold showers, aerobics and bracing music, advocated by some, are a bit strenuous for the seriously depressed, although, in fairness, the idea is more that such a lifestyle might prevent, rather than relieve, depression. 'Organic' foods (without preservatives or artificial colouring), vitamin supplements, ginseng and oil of evening primrose are in vogue, but costly. It helps some plump, mildly depressed people to lose a bit of weight – they feel fitter and more attractive and have a sense of mastery of their fate if they succeed – but there should be moderation in this as in most things: it does not help to develop a bulimic preoccupation with food and diet. Also sugar may be needed for the manufacture of serotonin in the body (which may be relevant to the taste for and even addiction to chocolate).

Pet 'therapy'

Having a pet helps depression. Pets keep you going, because they need to be fed and watered and, if dogs, exercised, and few depressed people will neglect their pets as much as they would themselves. Pets also act as confidantes. Cats and dogs are pretty good listeners, when in the mood, and though they may wander away for a sniff or a stretch, they return and do not butt in with premature advice. They are affectionate and show it. They do not turn away or pass judgement.

The term 'therapy' is not very appropriate. It will not help someone who is depressed to be given a pet, because it will be too much bother and the effort of adjusting to the presence of a new being is too much. The value of an established pet, on the other hand, is that it may speed recovery and prevent or delay relapse. Professor Elaine Murphy, of Guy's Hospital, London, is among those who have shown this.

Which pet? Dogs and cats are probably best because they are more responsive and cuddly than goldfish or caged birds. On the other hand they may die. Those who seek longevity are best advised to look for a parrot or a tortoise (although tortoises are not easily come by these days and can hardly be regarded as responsive by all save those who find any display of emotion deeply embarrassing).

This cat needs therapy - she tried to bite me..

Complementary therapies

The term 'complementary' means that the treatment may be given along with, rather than instead of ('alternative') more conventional treatments. The scientific basis for most complementary treatments is obscure, and the 'placebo' effect — benefit from the hopes raised by a new treatment, whether orthodox or 'way out' — must be high. Nevertheless, they are very popular (not least with the Royal Family).

Some of the practitioners (like acupuncturists and homeopaths) have a long, demanding training and these days doctors are less inclined to get on their high horse than they were, and readier to 'live and let live': "If you find it helpful, fine; I'll keep an open mind." Responsible complementary therapists are equally tolerant of orthodox medicine and psychiatry. However, it must be emphasised that no complementary therapies have been proven to be any good for severe depression.

Homeopathy

Although not a few homeopaths are medically qualified, the idea that giving really tiny amounts of substances which in larger quantities would mimic the symptoms of the disorder under treatment is a mystery to conventionally trained doctors. Nevertheless, many people with a horror of drugs find homeopathic remedies very appealing — and presumably they should not have too many side-effects. Also there is some scientific evidence that they may sometimes work. The elaborate system of homeopathy covers every ailment, certainly including depression (for which ignatia may be prescribed).

Acupuncture

This ancient Chinese system of healing, in which symptoms are relieved by needles inserted into selected points beneath the skin, has become better accepted by Western medicine than any other complementary technique. The sight (on film) of nonchalant, wide-awake Chinese having massive operations with only acupuncture for anaesthesia has persuaded most people that, if it is not an elaborate and surely pointless deception, it really works. Its main use is in the relief of pain, and there are 'rational' theories for how it might work: the stimulation of sensory nerves (those taking messages to the brain, like touch, temperature and, especially, pain) could release endorphins, the brain's natural pain-relievers (similar to opiates, like morphine). Opiates have, of course, effects on mood as well as pain (hence all the addiction), so acupuncture could well have a place in the treatment of depression. Not a few doctors, these days, have added acupuncture to their other skills.

The Bach flower remedies

Reading the indications for the special form of 'flower-power' developed by Dr Bach (pronounced 'batch', not like the composer) is like running through the symptoms of depression in Chapter 2 – What is depression? 'Mental torture behind 'brave face'', 'vague fears of unknown origin', 'fear of mind giving way', 'self-hatred – sense of uncleanliness', 'discouragement – despondency', 'hopelessness – despair', 'lack of confidence', 'deep gloom with no origin (black depression)', 'complete exhaustion', 'self-reproach – guilt', 'terror', 'uncertainty – indecision', 'extreme anguish', 'tenseness – hyperanxiety' are treated by, respectively, agrimony, aspen, cherry plum, crab apple, gentian, gorse, larch, mustard, olive, pine, rock rose, scleranthus, sweet chestnut and vervain. But let's hear it in particular for oak: 'despondent – but struggles on'!

Massage

The sensual pleasures of massage are obvious. How nice to lie down and be stroked and rubbed and gently pummelled, to have one's tense and aching muscles probed and kneaded! What could be more soothing? What could better encourage utter relaxation? What could be a more personal form of hands-on attention? It is a legitimised form of cuddling, which we may all crave from time to time although we think we should have outgrown it!

Massage alone is good enough, but it can be elaborated. Shiatsu is the circular massage of the pressure points used in acupuncture, with similar results. Aromatherapy involves the use of fragrant oils in the massage. Lymphatic massage purports to stimulate the lymphatic system and thus increase the body's immune defences. Reflexology is based on the extraordinary idea that all the parts of the body are represented on the palms and the soles, and treatment consists of a very thorough foot massage, with special attention to particular zones: the science may be suspect, but as a relaxing massage it's great!

14 The cost of depression

Cheer up - or I'm going to get DEPRESSED!

So far this book has made very plain the utter wretchedness of depression and the cost, in terms of suffering, to the individual. But what does it cost the community?

In human terms it costs those who are close to the patient a great deal. Next to suffering depression, the worst thing is enduring the depression of someone close to you, especially when it drags on and on. Chapter 8 indicates how families and friends may try to help those who are depressed, but this is no easy task when, for all one's patience, sympathy and encouragement, the sufferer keeps returning to his melancholy themes. Depressed people are emphatically 'no fun any more'. They can not only be miserable but morose – putting everyone else down as well as themselves and biting off the heads of their nearest and dearest. "Why doesn't Dad play with us anymore?" "Whatever happened to sex? I'm thinking of applying to a monastery!"

Being unfit to work may mean that the depressed person is around home far more than usual, but not enjoying it a bit. Marital tensions rise, and sometimes lead to separation and divorce. There is less money coming in. Women with prolonged post-natal depression (PND) look after their babies as a duty, rather than a pleasure. It is a terrible effort, and there is little time or inclination to delight in the baby's development – smiling, sitting up, clapping hands, saying 'Dad-dad-dad' and starting to crawl. Without the 'positive feedback' of the mother's pleasure and approval, these babies are measurably held back in their emotional and intellectual development at the age of three or four years. And should the depression tragically end in suicide – well, that is a deep wound which few families survive without a deep scar.

What about the cost to the National Health Service? One in five admissions to a psychiatric ward is for depression, costing £250 million at 1990 prices. There are three and a half million consultations with doctors in England and Wales every year, costing about £30 million. The cost of the prescriptions they write for antidepressants is £55 million – or more than £1 million a week!

Then there are the costs to society from loss of productivity from people who are depressed, either

The Cost of Depression..

because they are less efficient or off sick. One estimate by the Mental Health Foundation was that the total cost to the nation of mental illness in 1989 was almost £7000 million (what the Americans would call £7 billion), including social services, sickness and invalidity benefits, National Health Service treatment and care and lost production to business and industry. However, there was no separate estimate of the cost of depression. In the USA, however, it was estimated that the cost of depression alone was about £8 billion a year, and that three-quarters of these costs were due to loss of social and economic productivity and only a quarter to treatment. So earlier and better treatment could save a huge amount of money, as well as personal suffering.

What are the possible benefits of depression?

A psychologist recently caused a stir when he suggested that happiness was a pathological disorder. He was not referring to mania, which is evidently abnormal, but to that state of well being, love of our fellow man (and woman), cheerfulness and optimism which we generally regard as ideal.

It has already been suggested in this book that such a state is hardly justified by a realistic view of life, especially since the loss of a firm religious faith by so many (at least, in Western society) offers nothing to which to look forward in a life hereafter either. It is not true that 'they all lived happily ever after'. At best, they lived a long while, grew old and died, in various stages of infirmity, discomfort and loneliness. But if we were all aware at all times of our mortality, that the only certain thing in life is death, that we came out of oblivion and are almost certainly rushing back there, that all we achieve in this life is insignificant and rapidly forgotten, that life, as that wise and mellow poet and dramatist Christopher Fry put it is "the way we fatten for the Michaelmas of our own particular gallows", — why, there would be no point in our getting up in the morning! We might as well stay in our beds and rot! Why should we strive when life is full of wars, outrages, calamities, cruelties which confound our moral and artistic aspirations, and lessons never learnt? Those of us, like Brice and Mel, who were around while the Nazis were sending Jews to the gas chambers, had not expected in our own lifetime to find 'ethnic cleansing' in Bosnia in the 1990s.

Yet — "Hope springs eternal in the human heart!" Our astonishing optimism — "Never say die!" — enables us to suspend disbelief in our ultimate doom. Instead of resignation to the 'Grim Reaper', living every day as if it were our last, we act as if we were immortal – at least, until some nasty intimation of mortality, like the death of a friend or a heart attack or stroke, forces us to face the shortness of our future.

We have "eaten of the fruit of the Tree of Knowledge", yet we act as if we could not believe our eyes (or taste-buds)! Presumably this gives us an 'evolutionary advantage'? We survive as a species because of our irrational belief that we will survive as individuals!

But could there be any 'evolutionary advantage' in being depressed? Well, supposing our optimism was without bounds? Supposing nothing ever discouraged us? Supposing we would never 'let go' of what we had lost? Why, then might we not wear ourselves out in pursuing lost causes? Depression, perhaps, tells us when a cause is lost. It stops us from pursuing the unattainable. It balances the optimism which also helps us survive as a species.

This, of course, refers to normal depression. Sometimes the normal process of repairing and making good parts of the body during our fairly long lives is perverted into the rapid multiplication of cells, invading the local tissues of the body and spreading, by way of the bloodstream and lymph channels, to other parts, which we call cancer. Likewise normal emotions can get out of hand, and become exaggerated and caricatured in the form of our old enemies – mania and depressive illness.

15 Defeat depression!

In this last chapter it is time to review how to defeat depression. This really means preventing depression. To most people that will mean stopping it from happening in the first place, or primary prevention. However, there are other forms of prevention:

(a) early recognition and speedy, effective treatment, so that it is dispelled as quickly as possible (secondary prevention)
(b) helping people whose depression does not go away completely nevertheless to live as full lives as possible (tertiary prevention).

How can we stop depression from happening in the first place? The answer is, alas, 'not easily, nor often'. It cannot be denied that the 'gloom and doom' of a prolonged economic recession is likely to contribute to the increase in young male suicides in the UK, (interestingly in times of war, when the enemy is clearly defined and outside the community, suicide rates drop strikingly), but this is only amenable to political action. On the other hand, there is a fall in suicide rates in older men and women which might result from Britain's well-developed psychogeriatric services, in which Britain still leads the world.

Most of the causes listed in Chapter 6 cannot be avoided. It is an excellent idea to choose one's parents, but we do not know anyone who has found the trick of it! We cannot choose our gender, either, although it has been suggested that schoolgirls should be better educated about what to expect of combining marriage, motherhood and a career. (It appears, incidentally, that for mothers to choose to go out to work does protect against depression, but to have to go out to work to make ends meet may add to the depression.) Probably avoiding childbirth altogether would reduce a woman's risk of getting depressed, but of course that would rob many of an experience they crave, and it would not do

My day starts before I'm ready for it..

RING!
RING!

much for our species. (Marriage is said to be beneficial to men, but to put women's mental health in jeopardy. However, this is almost certainly because married women are (or were) more likely to have babies than single women, and not because of their oppressive husbands.) Teaching women (and men) how to be more assertive might reduce the numbers of those who feel frustrated and rendered helpless by the complexities and vagaries of modern life.

The best way to avoid, or delay, physical infirmity is by a healthy lifestyle, as mentioned under 'Mens sana in corpore sano' in Chapter 13 (p. 98). Sensible eating, moderate drinking and plenty of exercise are especially important. But Bernard Shaw observed, shrewdly, that this saying is the wrong way round: a healthy body is likely to result from a healthy mind!

Alcoholism and over-eating are often the consequence of unhappiness.

The worst effects of bereavement are avoidable by anticipatory grieving. It has been found, for example, that women who grieve in advance for the womb or breast they will have to lose cope much better afterwards than those who close their minds to the impending loss until it has actually happened. The same technique can be applied where the death of a loved one, say from cancer or motor neurone disease, is predictable.

Influenza vaccines are now readily available, and could and should be given to anyone who has a depressive tendency, thus reducing debility and disability from depressive and other post-viral syndromes.

The great obstacle to secondary prevention is stigma. If only the many, many famous, distinguished, immensely capable people who have suffered from depression would 'come out of the closet' and say so, how many more people would be encouraged to admit that they too felt depressed, and seek help early rather than very late in the day, if at all! Spike Milligan, a brilliant comedian and an outstandingly original writer, has had the courage to admit that he suffers from manic—depression, but how many others will do so? Esther Rantzen enabled many women to consider the possibility that they might have post-natal depression when she stated that she had experienced a mild form of the disorder, but how many of the hundreds and thousands of well-known women who have had the same experience will acknowledge it?

The truth is that stigma is real and injurious. We have hardly advanced in this respect since Biblical days, when mental illness was regarded as possession by devils. Michael Dukakis' chances of gaining the Presidency of the USA for the Democrats were dashed when it was revealed that he had been successfully treated for depression: why? Employment prospects are diminished and insurance premiums frequently increased by the acknowledgement of having had depression: why isn't this stamped on as vigorously as racism, sexism or any other unjust discrimination?

Small wonder, then, that patients resist the psychiatric label, and especially its confirmation by their actually seeing a psychiatrist. (Neurologists see many depressed people; although their training in no way equips them to treat them as well as psychiatrists, they have the immense advantage of not being psychiatrists. Imagine a world in which it was so shameful to see a stomach specialist that people preferred to be referred to an ear, nose and throat surgeon instead!)

There is nothing in the least disgraceful about suffering from depression. It has as much relationship to general ability and moral worth as appendicitis. It is a more serious illness, true, but one which can be most effectively treated. Yet more than half of those who suffer from it never even approach their general practitioners. So the most important way of defeating depression is by persuading them to do so. This means a huge public education exercise, first to explain what depression is, secondly that it is treatable and worth treating, and thirdly that it could and should be taken to the doctor.

However, at present general practitioners are quite likely either to miss depression or not take it seriously. So the first goal of the combined Defeat Depression Campaign of the Royal Colleges of Psychiatrists and General Practitioners has been to educate general practitioners in the recognition and treatment of depression: after all, many will only have learnt about it, and then probably in its most severe forms, for a week or two at medical school, often many years ago. All members of the Royal College of General Practitioners were sent in mid-1993 an excellent book by Dr Alastair Wright, while at the same time the Department of Health sent a booklet entitled 'Defeat Depression' to every general practice in the country, as part of their drive to improve the management of mental illness and reduce suicide rates as part of a campaign called *The Health of the Nation*.

The value of such education has been shown by research in the Swedish island of Gotland, where an intensive campaign on depression and its treatment was begun for the general practitioners in 1993. After this there were fewer absences with sick leave for depression, prescriptions for tranquillisers, sedatives and sleeping-tablets decreased, in-patient treatment for depression dwindled by two-thirds and the frequency of suicide was reduced significantly. However, three years after the end of the educational project, figures were very nearly back to how they had been before. So, if education was responsible for these remarkable improvements, it needs to be continuous and not 'one-off'.

What is the best form of treatment? Interestingly, simple recognition of the depression counts for quite a lot. Psychiatrists Dr Lester Sireling and Professor Gene Paykel and general practitioner Professor Paul Freeling showed that patients whose major depression had gone unrecognised were more ill, felt and looked more depressed, were more irritable and suffered more loss of energy and appetite than did those whose depression had been recognised, despite the fact that most of the latter had not taken any treatment.

Counselling seems to be the treatment most patients want, although they may not be fully aware of its limitations: it is not effective alone for more than very moderate depression; skilled, trained counsellors are needed but are variably available; and patients themselves must make a commitment – of time, patience, sometimes money and the readiness to look at their true feelings. So this means: (a) training more people to be counsellors; and (b) public education in reasonable expectations.

Counselling may be enough in itself, or may need to lead on to more sophisticated psychological treatments like cognitive therapy and dynamic psychotherapy.

Is it safe to come out today?

Again, these skills are thin on the ground, notably outside London; if they are to be made more widely available in the 'brave new world' of Britain's 'reformed' health services, 'purchasers' will have to be persuaded of their value.

Counselling alone will not do for more severe depression, and a great deal needs to be taught to the public about the safety and effectiveness of antidepressants. Princess Diana, who should have been better advised, recently lumped together tranquillisers, sleeping tablets and antidepressants as drugs causing subservience (to their apparent lot in life) and dependency, especially in women. It needs, apparently, to be shouted again and again from the housetops: ANTIDEPRESSANTS ARE NOT ADDICTIVE!

They are not at all the same as tranquillisers, any more than antibiotics are the same as analgesics (pain-relievers). They do not usually work for three weeks, but after that time they generally do, and can then be continued for months without any risk of dependency.

Yet Dr John Henry from Guy's Hospital has calculated that only one depressed person in 20 in Britain at present benefits from antidepressant treatment. This is mainly because the drugs are never prescribed, but also because they are not taken – at all, or for long enough – or because the dose is inadequate.

Clearly, then, the public needs far more education and persuasion in the taking of antidepressants when they are needed. The present drugs are pretty good, but in the future we should hope for rather different antidepressants, instead of 'more of the same'. There are now many antidepressants said to be more easily tolerated and safer than their predecessors, but few have been shown to be more effective (except when fewer of the less tolerable side-effects leads to better compliance). The great need is for a fast-acting antidepressant, effective and easy to take, which will have the patient fully back to normal life in a month. At present it appears that those who have needed to take an antidepressant at all need to go on taking it for longer after they have recovered than had been supposed if they are not to relapse – for at least six months in younger people, and more than two years in older.

We also need to educate doctors and their patients in the use of lithium carbonate: it has improved the outlook for severe and recurrent depression so much that less electroconvulsive therapy need now be given. At the same time we need to demystify electroconvulsive therapy and support its use for severe depression, at least until something as good has been found to take its place. Sometimes it requires courage from psychiatrists to go on giving so unpopular a treatment in the 'teeth of so much popular prejudice'. But at the same time we must respect the rights of patients to refuse such treatment, unless they are seriously mentally ill and their lives are in danger.

The public needs to be aware of times when the risk of depression is high and when the possibility that this is what is wrong needs careful consideration. They include:

(a) having a baby
(b) being made redundant
(c) having been mugged or burgled
(d) in the throes of marital troubles
(e) after a bereavement
(f) after 'flu
(g) after a more serious illness, like a heart attack or stroke.

Most people, fortunately, will never encounter suicide, but it is as well to be aware of when the risk is high. This is when:

(a) depression is severe
(b) depression is accompanied by serious physical illness (like cancer)
(c) the person is talking of suicide

(d) there is a dire life-situation like bereavement, redundancy, serious debt or facing criminal proceedings

(e) there has been a past attempt at suicide

(f) there has been suicide in the family.

To avert suicide in those at risk, family and friends need to be vigilant and in touch with the primary health care team: the general practitioner, practice nurse, health visitor, community psychiatric nurse, psychologist and/or social worker. There must also be ready action, expertise and adequate resources (including a speedy consultation, in the patient's home, and a bed, if need be) from the local psychiatric service.

Just send in someone to do my suffering...

"What started to make me better was when my GP gave me a special appointment that week and gave me time to talk. I felt I was being allowed to be ill, and taken seriously. He said he'd arrange for me to see a counsellor in the practice, but there'd be a bit of a wait, and would I like antidepressant tablets for a while? Would I? Anything to make me better, so I went on this – tricyclic? Anyway it was round and red and I started with one at night, then two. They made my mouth dry at first – the doctor said that that was a sign that they were working.

Then he asked me a bit about how I'd coped when my own father died six years ago. Well, I'd coped brilliantly – I didn't cry, or anything, but that was because it just didn't seem real. And then my wife's Dad died, quite suddenly a few weeks ago, and I was sobbing like a fool at the funeral – like a fool because I was never all that crazy about him. When I saw the counsellor we talked a bit more about life at home, mainly when I was a kid. I had to admit that my father had been a bit of an old swine – well, they were pretty strict in those days, Dads – I don't suppose he was any worse than the others. Anyway, I found that I loved him – it may sound corny, like one of those awful American films, but that's how I felt. Poor old Dad! Poor me – we never had a real heart-to-heart, but talking with the counsellor brought it all back.

Why's this important? I asked her. It's got nothing to do with my life now. Never mind, she said, I expect it was your father-in-law dying that brought it back to you. Anyway, it seems to be what you want to talk about. Yes, I said, well Grace had such a lovely relationship with her Dad and Mum that I felt quite envious at times. Anyway, I'm starting to feel better now. I think it's the talking, my doctor says it's the tablets, and my mate Joe says it's time – the Great Healer, he says."

Appendix 1

Assessing depression. From Dr Zigmond and Dr Snaith's Hospital Anxiety and Depression Scale

(2) I still enjoy the things I used to enjoy
   Definitely as much
   Not quite as much
   Only a little
   Hardly at all

(4) I can still laugh and see the funny side of things
   As much as I always could
   Not quite as much now
   Definitely not so much now
   Not at all

(6) I feel cheerful
   Most of the time
   Sometimes
   Not often
   Not at all

(8) I feel as if I am slowed down
   Not at all
   Sometimes
   Very often
   Nearly all the time

(10) I have lost interest in my appearance
   I take as much care as ever
   I may not take quite as much care
   I don't take as much care as I should
   Definitely

---

(12) I look forward with enjoyment to things
   As much as I ever did
   Rather less than I used to
   Definitely less than I used to
   Hardly at all

(14) I can enjoy a good book or radio or TV programme
   Often
   Sometimes
   Not often
   Very seldom

Appendix 2

Useful addresses

Association for Post-Natal Illness

25 Jerdan Place, Fulham,
London SW6 1BE
Tel: 071—386 0868
Women who have survived post-natal depression help
women who are suffering from it.

The British Association for Counselling

1 Regent Place, Rugby, Warwickshire CV21 3BX
Tel: 0788—578328
Helps you to find counsellors.

Cruse Bereavement Care

126 Sheen Road, Richmond, Surrey TW9 1UR
Tel: 081—940 4818
Help for the widowed.

Depressives Anonymous

36 Chestnut Avenue, Beverley,
North Humberside HU17 9QU
Tel: 0482—860619
Support for sufferers.

Depressives Associated

PO Box 1022, London SE1 7QB
Tel: 081—760 0544
Information for sufferers.

The Manic—Depressive Fellowship

8—10 High Street, Kingston upon Thames, Surrey
KT1 1EY
Tel: 081—974 6550
For manic—depressives and those who support them.

Mental Health Foundation

37 Mortimer Street, London W1N 7RJ
Tel: 071–580 0145
Information about mental illness, funds research.

MIND (National Association for Mental Health)

22 Harley Street, London W1N 2ED
Tel: 071–637 0741
Information and advocacy.

Relate (National Marriage Guidance)

HQ Office, Herbert Gray College, Little Church Street, Rugby CV21 3AP
Tel: 0788–573241
Counselling for the married and those in sexual partnerships.

Royal College of Psychiatrists

17 Belgrave Square,
London SW1X 8PG
Tel: 071–235 2351
Information about mental illness and psychiatry.

SAD Association

PO Box 989, London SW7 2PZ
Tel: 081–969 7028
Support and advice for sufferers from seasonal affective disorder.

The Samaritans

46 Marshall Street, London W1V 1LR
Tel: 071–734 2800
Support the suicidal. Have 184 branches nationwide, open all day every day. Look for your local branch in the telephone book.

Westminster Pastoral Foundation

23 Kensington Square, London W8 5HN
Tel: 071–937 6956
Trains counsellors and provides a counselling service.

Good reading

Darkness Visible. By WILLIAM STYRON. London: Jonathan Cape Ltd. 1991.

Defeat Depression. By the ROYAL COLLEGE OF PSYCHIATRISTS IN ASSOCIATION WITH THE ROYAL COLLEGE OF GENERAL PRACTITIONERS. London: Department of Health. 1993.

Depression. By PAUL HAUCK. London: Sheldon Press. 1974.

Depression. By RICHARD WEST. London: Office of Health Economics. 1992.

Depression: Recognition & Management in General Practice. By ALASTAIR WRIGHT. London: Royal College of General Practitioners. 1993.

Depression and How to Survive It. By SPIKE MILLIGAN & ANTHONY CLARE. London: Ebury Press. 1993.

Moodswing. By RONALD R. FIEVE. London: Bantam Books Ltd.

Psychogeriatrics. By BRICE PITT. Edinburgh: Churchill Livingstone. 1982.

Good listening

Control Your Tension. Lifeskills, 3 Brighton Road, London N2
Tel: 081—346 9646

The Mitchell Method of Relaxation. By LAURA MITCHELL. 8 Gainsborough Gardens, London NW3 1BJ

Index

Side-effects *see* drugs for depression, side-effects
Sinequan *see* doxepin
Skinner, B.F.   72
Skynner, Dr Robin   69
Sleep: deprivation   97
   disorders   6, 11, 12, 28, 47, 51, 61
   tablets   76
   treatment   96
'Slough of Despond'   2
Smiling depression   *see* classification of depression
Smoking   56
Snaith, Dr (*see* HAD)   ix, 20, 114—115
'Snake Pit', The   91
Social class   17, 53
   support   54, 59—62
   workers   33, 60, 112
Sodium   85
'Split' thinking   70
Stereotaxis   94
Steroid drugs   39
Stigma   33, 108
Stimulants   76
Stress   22, 39
Stroke   41, 79
Styron, William   3
Sugar   98
Suicidal, suicide   6, 12, 16, 28, 36, 44, 45, 56, 82, 109, 111, 112
Sullivan, Harry Stack   69
'Sundown' phenomenon   51
Surgeons   90
Surmontil *see* trimipramine
Sweating on tricyclic antidepressants   81

Sweet chestnut   101
Synapse   38, 79, 80, 85

Tax return   59
Tegretol *see* carbamazepine
Tension, muscular   47, 56
Therapeutic alliance   66
Therapist   66—70, 74
Thyroid gland   38, 51, 96
Thyrotoxicosis   38
Thyroxine   38, 52, 86, 89
Time, the healer   55, 113
Tofranil *see* imipramine
Tortoises as pets   99
Tranqillisers, major *see* neuroleptics; minor *see* benzodiazepines
Transference, in psychotherapy   67—69
'Tranx' *see* benzodiazepines
Tranylcypromine (Parnate)   79
Trazodone (Molipaxin)   83
Treatment of depression: drug *see* drugs for depression
   physical *see* physical treatments for depression
   psychological *see* psychological treatments for depression
'Tree of Knowledge'   105
Tremor on lithium   86
Tricyclics *see* drugs for depression
Trimipramine (Surmontil)   83, 89
Tryptizol *see* amitriptyline
Tube-feeding   43, 45
Tuberculosis   45, 78
Twin studies   29
Tyramine   79

Unconscious mind   64, 66
Unemployment and depression   17, 33, 41, 59
'Users'   61

Validity (of tests)   20
Valproate   87
Van Gogh   2
Varah, Rev. Chad   60
Vervain   101
Viral infections   42, 45, 53, 53, 108
Vision, blurring of on tricyclics   80
Vitamins   55, 98

Waking, early   11, 22, 77
Water, difficulty in passing on tricyclics   80
Weight gain on antidepressants   81, 84, 86
   loss in depression   11, 22, 27, 49, 51, 72
Wickedness, delusions of   24, 50
Widowing   45, 61
Witches   2
Women and depression   17, 30, 39
Woolf, Virginia   3
Wright, Dr Alastair   110

X-chromosome   31

Y-chromosome   31
Yeast extracts   79
'Yuppy 'flu' *see* myalgic encephalitis (ME)

Zigmond, Dr (*see* HAD)   ix, 20, 114—115